Instructor's Manual

to accompany

International Economics

Eleventh Edition

Thomas Pugel
New York University

Peter Lindert
UC Davis

Irwin McGraw-Hill

Boston   Burr Ridge, IL   Dubuque, IA   Madison, WI   New York   San Francisco   St. Louis
Bangkok   Bogotá   Caracas   Lisbon   London   Madrid
Mexico City   Milan   New Delhi   Seoul   Singapore   Sydney   Taipei   Toronto

McGraw-Hill Higher Education

A Division of The McGraw-Hill Companies

Instructor's Manual to accompany
INTERNATIONAL ECONOMICS

1 2 3 4 5 6 7 8 9 0 HAM/HAM 9 0 9 8 7 6 5 4 3 2 1 0 9

ISBN 0-07-290388-0

http://www.mhhe.com

Contents

Chapter 1

International Economics Is Different

Overview

The introduction to the subject of international economics has three major purposes:
1. Show that international economics addresses important and interesting current events and issues.
2. Show why international economics is special.
3. Provide a broad overview of the book.

We begin with four sets of events that show the importance of current issues addressed by international economics. The first is a set of trade policy conflicts. Here we introduce the rising importance of regional trade agreements (trade blocs) and the role of the World Trade Organization (WTO) as a global arbiter. One policy conflict is the fight over the European Union's banana import policy. The WTO ruling went against the European Union, and the WTO allowed the United States to retaliate with 100 percent tariffs on specific products. Another policy conflict is the European Union's refusal to import beef raised using growth hormones. Again, the WTO ruling went against the European Union.

The second is the set of financial crises that hit the world economy. We trace the beginning of the crisis in Thailand in 1997 and the subsequent contagion that spread to other Asian countries that year, as well as effects on countries outside Asia, including Russia in 1998. We summarize five diagnoses showing the range of opinion about what caused the crises and what can be done in response.

The third is European monetary union, in which 11 of the 15 European Union countries are in the process of replacing their national moneys with a single new currency, the euro. The monetary union has been controversial, because countries must yield powers over national monetary policy to the new unionwide European Central Bank.

The fourth is the set of controversies over policy toward immigration. Industrialized countries impose limits on legal immigration, and there are pressures to tighten the limits and to do more to stop illegal immigration. Addressing concerns about the fiscal effects of immigration, the U. S. government in 1996 passed a law to make even legal immigrants ineligible for some government benefits and services.

These four sets of events show that international economics addresses important current issues. They also can be used to show why international economics is special—why national boundaries matter in economics. The first reason that international economics is special is that national government policies matter—in fact, they matter in two ways. One way is that national governments adopt policies toward international transactions. This is seen clearly in the

1

discussions of bananas, beef, and immigration, as well as in the diagnosis that capital controls can prevent or limit financial crises. The other way is that national governments adopt different macroeconomic policies. These national policies usually are designed to serve national interests, but they often have international effects. The tension between national interests and international effects is raised in the diagnoses of financial crises that focus on flawed financial systems and the need to tighten the government budget. Tension is also seen in the controversy over ceding national monetary authority to European monetary union.

The second reason that international economics is special is that some resources do not move freely between countries. Land is essentially immobile. There are substantial impediments to the movement of labor internationally, because the personal and economic costs to people of moving from one country to another can be substantial. As the discussion of immigration shows, government policies also often impede international movement of labor. Financial capital moves more freely, but, as the discussion of financial crises shows, international capital movements can sometimes be surprisingly disruptive.

Tips for teaching

One good way to begin the first class session is with a look at current events, even before the mechanics and requirements of the course are presented. The instructor might use the day's newspaper (for instance, the *Financial Times* or *Wall Street Journal*) or the week's magazine (for instance, the *Economist* or *Business Week*) to highlight a few stories related to the content of the course. We have found that this is good way to get the students' attention and interest. Another good beginning would be to provide a discussion that updates one or more of the four sets of events in Chapter 1. For example, the instructor could look at the how the value of the euro has moved in recent months or since its birth.

You may want to consider beginning every class session of the course (not only the first class session) with a look at one or two stories in that day's newspaper. The stories should relate in some way to the material covered in the course, but they do have to relate to the specific material covered in that day's session. We have found that this look at current events reinforces the relevance of international economic analysis. It also encourages students to read a good newspaper or magazine and to keep up with current events. In addition, we can model critical reading, if we both summarize the article's information and offer our own opinion or analysis (or ask the students for their opinions).

The instructor may also point out that there is a lot of information on international issues available on the World Wide Web. Figure A.1 in Appendix A provides a list of some important sites.

Chapter 2

The Basic Theory of International Trade
Demand and Supply

Overview

This chapter indicates why we study theories of international trade and presents the basic theory using supply and demand curves. Trade is important to individual consumers, to workers and other factor owners, to firms, and therefore to the whole economy. Trade is also controversial, with perpetual battles over government policies toward trade. To understand all of this, we need to develop theories of why people trade as they do.

It is useful to organize the analysis of international trade by contrasting a world of no trade with a world of free trade, leaving analysis of intermediate cases (e.g., non-prohibitive tariffs) for Part II. The analysis seeks to answer four key questions about international trade:
1. Why do countries trade? What determines the pattern of trade?
2. How does trade affect production and consumption in each country?
3. What are the gains (or losses) for a country as a whole from trading?
4. What are the effects of trade on different groups in a country? Are there groups that gain and other groups that lose?

Theories of international trade provide answers to these four questions.

Basic demand and supply analysis can be used to provide early answers to these four questions, as well as to introduce concepts that can be used in more elaborate theories. Using motorbikes as an example, the chapter first reviews the basic analysis of both demand (the demand curve, other influences on quantity demanded, movements along the demand curve and shifts in the demand curve, and the price elasticity of demand as a measure of responsiveness) and supply (the supply curve, the role of marginal cost, other influences on quantity supplied, movements along the supply curve and shifts in the supply curve, and the price elasticity of supply). It pays special attention to the meaning and measurement of consumer surplus and producer surplus. This section, which focuses on review and development of basic tools, ends with the picture of market equilibrium in a national market with no trade as the intersection of the domestic demand curve and the domestic supply curve.

The remainder of the chapter examines the use of supply and demand curves to analyze international trade. If there are two international markets and no trade, it is likely that the product's price will differ between the two markets. Someone should notice the difference and try to profit by arbitrage between the two markets. If governments permit free trade, then the export supply from the initially low-priced market (the rest of the world in the textbook example) can satisfy the import demand in the initially high-priced market (the United States in the textbook example), and the world shifts to a free-trade equilibrium. We can show this free trade equilibrium by deriving the supply-of-exports curve for the rest of the world and the demand-for-imports curve for the United States. The international market for the product clears at the intersection of the export-supply and import-demand curves, indicating the equilibrium international or world price and the quantity traded. This equilibrium world price also becomes the domestic price in each country with free trade.

The same set of three graphs (the two national markets and the international-trade market) is used to show the effects of the shift from no-trade to free-trade on different groups in each country and to show the net gains from trade for each nation. In the importing country consumers of the product gain consumer surplus and producers of the product lose producer surplus. Using the one-dollar, one-vote yardstick, the country as a whole gains, because the gain in consumer surplus is larger than the loss of producer surplus. In the exporting country producers of the product gain producer surplus and consumers of the product lose consumer surplus. Furthermore, the analysis shows that the country as a whole gains because the gain in producer surplus is larger than the loss of consumer surplus. The country that gains more from the shift to free trade is the country whose price changes more--the country with the less elastic trade curve (import demand or export supply).

Tips

We believe that this chapter is an excellent way to introduce the analysis of trade. The four questions about trade focus student attention on key issues that are interesting to most of them. Students then get a quick payoff through the use of the familiar supply-demand framework. By the end of this short chapter we have preliminary answers to all four trade questions. We have also laid a solid foundation for the analysis of trade using supply and demand curves, the approach that will receive the most attention in Part II on trade policies.

In class presentations it may be useful to show the graphs in a sequence, perhaps using a series of overhead slides. After presenting the review of demand and supply and the national market equilibrium with no trade, the following sequence works well.

1. Two national market graphs with no trade, one with a high no-trade price (the United States), and one with a low no-trade price (the rest of the world, or ROW). Question to the class: "If you were the first person to notice this situation, could you make a profit?" This is a good way to motivate international trade driven by arbitrage.
2. The U.S. national market graph and the international market graph. Question to the class: "Let's say that the United States is willing to open up to free trade and integrate into the world market. If it does this, the world price will also be the price within the United States. How much will the United States want to import?" It depends on what the world price is. The instructor can pick one or two hypothetical world price(s) (below the no-trade U.S. price), and measure the gap between domestic quantity demanded and domestic quantity supplied. This is the U.S. demand for imports, and these import quantity-price combinations can be used to plot the U.S. demand-for-imports curve in the international market.
3. A graph of the international market and the ROW national market. A comparable discussion to item 2 above, to derive the supply-of-exports curve.
4. Superimpose the graphs from item 2 on the graphs from item 3. Question to the class: "What will happen with free trade? When there is ongoing free trade, what is the equilibrium world price?" (After superimposing the two sets of graphs, it is probably useful to replace them

with a single new set of the same three graphs, to remove the clutter that came with deriving the demand-for-imports and supply-of-exports curves.) This set of three graphs can be used to show the free-trade equilibrium: world price, quantity traded, and quantities produced and consumed in each country.

5. A single graph showing the U.S. national market, to contrast no trade with free trade. Questions to the class: "What group is made happier by the shift from no trade to free trade? What group is a loser? Can we somehow say that the country gains from free trade?"

6. A single graph showing the ROW national market, with the same questions in item 5.

Subsequent chapters in Part I present additional theories of trade. The figure shown on the accompanying page provides a summary of the key features of these theories. It may be useful to copy and distribute this figure to your students. If it is distributed when the class begins to study the material, it can serve as a roadmap. If it is distributed when the class finishes the lectures on the material, it can serve as a summary and review.

For instructors who want to begin with the discussion of absolute and comparative advantage rather than with the supply-and-demand framework that focuses on a single product, this should be possible. After covering the introductory material (the first two pages of Chapter 2), the course would skip to Chapter 3. The remaining material from Chapter 2 on the supply and demand analysis can be inserted right after Chapter 3's section referring to analysis using supply and demand curves, or this material can be presented as a separate topic elsewhere in the course.

Suggested answers to questions and problems

(in the textbook)

2. Producer surplus is the net gain to producers from being able to sell a product through a market. It is the difference between the lowest price at which some producer is willing to supply each unit of the product and the actual market price that is paid, summed over all units that are produced and sold. The lowest price at which someone is willing to supply the unit just covers the extra (marginal) cost of producing that unit. To measure producer surplus for a product using real world data, three major pieces of information are needed. First, the market price. Second, the quantity supplied. Third, some information about the slope (or shape) of the supply curve. How would quantity supplied change if the market price decreased? Or, what are the extra costs of producing each unit up to the actual quantity supplied? Producer surplus could then be measured as the area below the market price line and above the supply curve.

4. The country's demand for imports is the amount by which the country's domestic quantity demanded exceeds the country's domestic quantity supplied. The demand-for-imports curve is derived by finding the difference between domestic quantity demanded and domestic quantity supplied, for each possible market price for which quantity demanded exceeds quantity supplied. The demand-for-imports curve shows the quantity that the country would want to import for each possible international market price.

6. If there were no exports of scrap iron and steel, the domestic market would clear at the price at which domestic quantity demanded equals domestic quantity supplied. But the

United States does export scrap iron and steel. The extra demand from foreign buyers increases the market price of scrap iron and steel. Domestic users of scrap iron and steel pay a higher price than they would if there were no exports. Thus, some support a prohibition on these exports, in order to lower the market price of the scrap that they buy.

8. a. With free trade at $18 per barrel:
Domestic production Q_S: $18 = 0.6 + 6Q_S$, or $Q_s = 2.9$ billion barrels.
Domestic consumption Q_D: $18 = 42 - 4Q_D$, or $Q_D = 6$ billion barrels.

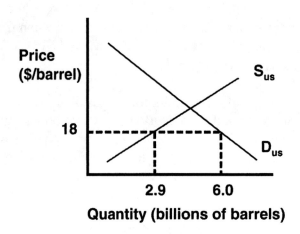

b. With no imports, domestic quantity supplied must equal domestic quantity demanded (both equal to Q_N) at the domestic equilibrium price P:
$42 - 4Q_N = 0.6 + 6Q_N$, or $Q_N = 4.14$ billion barrels produced and consumed.
Using one of the equations, we can calculate that the domestic price would be $25.44 per barrel.

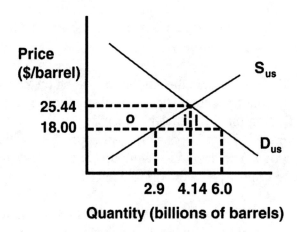

6

c. Domestic producers of oil would gain, receiving an increase of producer surplus shown as area o in the graph. Domestic consumers of oil would lose, experiencing a loss of consumer surplus shown as area o + i + l in the graph.

10. The supply curve S_{US} shifts down (or to the right). The U.S. demand-for-imports curve D_m shifts to the left (or down). The equilibrium international price decreases below 1,000--it is shown by the intersection of the new U.S. D_m curve and the original S_x curve.

12. a. In the graphs below, the free trade equilibrium price is P_F, the price at which the quantity of exports supplied by Country I equals the quantity of imports demanded by Country II. (The quantity-of-imports demanded curve for country II is the same as the country's regular demand curve.) This world price is above the no-trade price in country I. The quantity traded with free trade is Q_T.

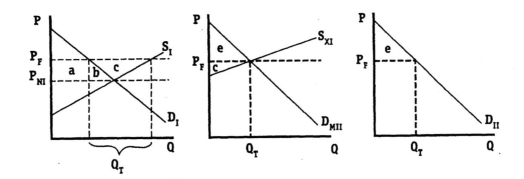

b. In Country I producer surplus increases by area a + b + c, and consumer surplus falls by area a + b. The net national gain from free trade is area c. In country II consumer surplus increases by area e and this is also the net national gain from trade. Because there is no domestic production in Country II with or without trade, there is no change in producer surplus.

A guide to the trade theories of Part One

Name of Theory	What Forces Determine Trade Flows?	Some Key Assumptions
A. The basic theory (Chapters 2-5)	Productivities Factor Supplies Product demands	Competition in all markets Constant or increasing costs Any number of production factors (types of labor, land, etc.)
B. Supply-oriented theories of trade (special cases of the basic theory, with the demand side neutral):		
1. Absolute advantage (in Chapter 3)	Absolute productivities	Competition in all markets Constant marginal costs Only one factor (labor)
2. Comparative advantage (in Chapter 3)	Relative productivities	Competition in all markets Constant marginal costs Only one factor (labor)
3. Factor proportions (Heckscher-Ohlin theory, in Chapters 3-5)	Relative factor endowments	Competition in all markets Increasing marginal costs Small number of factors Technology neutral
C. Alternative theories of trade:		
1. Technology differences, including product cycle (Vernon and others, in Chapter 5)	Technological innovation Technological "age" of the industry	Competition Importance of research and development
2. Monopolistic competition (Krugman and others, in Chapter 6)	Product differentiation Moderate scale economies	Imperfect competition De-emphasize factor supplies
3. Global oligopoly (in Chapter 6)	Substantial internal scale economies History, luck, or government policy	Imperfect competition De-emphasize factor supplies
4. External economies (in Chapter 6)	Substantial external scale economies Large home market, history, luck, or government policy	Competition De-emphasize factor supplies

Chapter 3

Why Everybody Trades
Comparative Advantage and Factor Proportions

Overview

This chapter extends the analysis of international trade to consider trade in a multiple-product economy. An economy composed of two products is useful to bring out insights about international trade. This general equilibrium approach explicitly shows the effects of resource reallocations between industries. The chapter shows how our understanding of trade, especially of why countries trade, has evolved over time.

The story begins with Adam Smith and absolute advantage. (A box on mercantilism summarizes the view that Smith opposed and shows how mercantilist thinking continues today.) The analysis focuses on the resource cost (labor hours) of producing each of two products (wheat and cloth) in two countries (the United States and the rest of the world). Smith examined the case of absolute advantage in which the labor hours to produce one product are lower in one country and the labor hours to produce the other product are lower in the other country. The resource costs (or labor hour input-output coefficients) indicate the relative prices of the products in each country with no trade. The difference in prices with no trade sets up the opportunity for arbitrage, with each good being exported from the initially low-price country and imported by the initially high-price country. The shift to a free trade equilibrium results in an equilibrium international price. Without information on demand, we cannot say exactly what this price will be, but we do know that it is between the two no-trade price ratios.

Smith's approach does not indicate what would happen if the same country had absolute advantage in both products. Ricardo took up this case and demonstrated the principle of comparative advantage—a country will trade in the pattern that maximizes its advantage (or minimizes its disadvantage). With the exception that one country has an absolute advantage in both products, the example to demonstrate Ricardo's insight is very similar to the example used to illustrate Smith's insight.

The chapter uses the Ricardian example to introduce a key analytical device—the production possibility curve, which shows all combinations of outputs of different goods that an economy can produce with full employment of resources and maximum productivity. The resource costs of producing each product in the country and the total amount of labor hours available in the country are used to graph the country's production possibility curve, a straight line whose slope equals the (negative of the) extra (or marginal) cost of additional cloth. The straight line indicates that the marginal or opportunity cost of each good in each country is constant, following Ricardo's assumptions. The slope of this line also indicates the relative price of cloth (the good on the x-axis) with no trade.

If free trade results in an equilibrium international price ratio that is strictly between the two no-trade price ratios (because both countries are "large countries"), then each country specializes completely in producing only the good in which it has the comparative advantage. Each trades at the equilibrium international price ratio (along a trade line or price line) to reach its consumption point. Both countries gain from trade. Each is able to consume more of both goods than it consumed with no trade.

The assumption of constant marginal cost and the implication that countries will completely specialize in producing only one (or a few) product(s) are unrealistic. In the modern theory of international trade, we use the assumption of increasing marginal costs—as one industry expands at the expense of others, increasing amounts of other goods must be given up to obtain each extra unit of the expanding output. Increasing marginal cost results in a bowed-out production possibility curve. This is linked to upward-sloping supply curves for each product. Increasing marginal costs arise because some resources are better suited to producing one good rather than the other (including differences in factor input proportions between the two products—Appendix B shows this explicitly). The market price ratio determines which production point will actually be chosen. Production will be driven to levels at which the marginal (or opportunity) cost of producing another unit just equals the price at which the output can be sold. On the graph this is a tangency between the production possibility curve and the price line whose slope reflects the market price ratio.

The second key analytical tool that we need is a way to picture demand for two products at the same time. For individuals this can be done using indifference curves and income or budget lines. The chapter reviews (or summarizes) the basics of indifference curves (levels of well-being or happiness or utility, bowed shape, infinite number of which only a few are usually pictured). It then indicates that we are going to use community indifference curves, even though there are serious questions about them. At the least, they are reasonable for depicting national demand patterns for two goods simultaneously. Under certain assumptions they also provide information on national well-being or welfare, but this use is more debatable.

Putting the production possibility curve together with the community indifference curves results in a picture of an entire (two-product) economy. The chapter shows the equilibrium with no trade (a tangency of a community indifference curve with the production possibility curve). It then shows two countries whose no-trade price ratios differ. When trade is opened between the two countries, an equilibrium international price ratio is established that clears the international markets for the two goods. Production in each country shifts to the tangency with the new price line (whose slope shows the equilibrium international price), and each country trades along the price line to a consumption point determined by a tangency between the price line and a community indifference curve. The right-angle triangle between the production point and the consumption point is a trade triangle showing export and import quantities for each country. (The chapter also indicates how the graph can be used to derive a demand curve for cloth, so that the analysis is shown to be consistent with the supply-demand analysis from the previous chapter.)

The graph can be used to show that each country gains from trade. Trade allows each country to consume beyond its ability to produce (shown by the production possibility curve). Trade allows each country to reach a higher community indifference curve. How much the country gains from trade depends on the country's terms of trade—the price of its exports relative to the price of its imports. The graph also shows the effects on the production and consumption quantities for each good in each country.

The chapter ends by returning to the key question addressed in the chapter—what determines the pattern of trade. While demand differences might explain some trade, most analysis focuses on production-side differences. If demand is neutral, then the trade pattern is determined by production-side differences that cause no-trade price ratios to differ. In our graph, these differences skew one country's production possibility curve toward producing wheat and the other country's toward producing cloth. The skewness itself could arise for two reasons. First, production technologies or resource productivities may differ between countries. This explanation is the one used in the Ricardian approach, and we will return to it in Chapter 5. But, for the remainder of this chapter and the next chapter, we ignore technology or resource productivity differences, and instead focus on the second reason—differences in resource availability and resource use.

The skewness of production possibility curves can arise because resource availability differs between countries and the use of these factors in producing differs between products. These differences in factor endowments and factor proportions lead to the Heckscher-Ohlin theory of trade patterns—countries export the products that use their abundant factors intensively (and import the products that use their scarce factors intensively). With no trade the relatively abundant production factors will be relatively cheap, so that the product that uses these factors relatively intensively will have a low no-trade price. As trade is opened, this product is exported.

Tips

This chapter presents the full sweep of the development of thinking about comparative advantage as an explanation of the pattern of trade, beginning with absolute advantage, continuing with comparative advantage according to Ricardo, and concluding with Heckscher and Ohlin's insight that comparative advantage can be based on differences in factor proportions and factor endowments. We believe that this is a major strength. Students can see the development as a progression rather than as separate theories. We also integrate the development of analytical tools, developing the production possibility curve and community indifference curves on a "just-in-time" basis.

However, this is also a long chapter relative to most others in the textbook. Some instructors may prefer to split the reading assignments for the chapter into two pieces. The first covers the absolute and comparative advantage of Smith and Ricardo. The second covers the Heckscher-Ohlin approach, including the analytical tools used in this approach—beginning with the section "Increasing Marginal Costs."

If you use offer curves to show the determination of the equilibrium international price ratio you can assign and cover the material in Appendix C.

Suggested answers to questions and problems
(in the textbook)

2.   Agree. Imports permit the country to consume more (or do more capital investment using imported capital goods). Anything that is exported is not available for domestic consumption (or capital investment). Although this loss is bad, exports are like a necessary evil because exports are how the country pays for the imports that it wants.

4.   For a given relative price of cloth, the quantity produced and supplied of cloth is shown by the point of tangency between the production possibility curve and a line with a slope equal to the (negative of the) relative price ratio. By varying the relative price of cloth, the quantities of cloth supplied at different relative prices can be determined, and these combinations graphed to produce a supply curve for cloth. The same procedure can be used to derive the supply curve for wheat. The quantity of wheat must be measured from the vertical axis in the production-possibility-curve graph, and the relative price of wheat is the reciprocal of the slope of the price line. (The supply curve for wheat is actually a curve, not a straight line, in this case.)

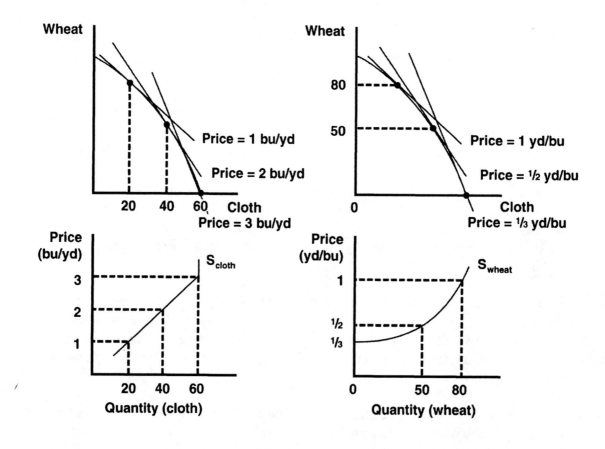

6.   For price ratios below 2 bushels per yard, the country exports wheat and imports cloth. As the price becomes lower, the quantity produced of cloth decreases and the quantity consumed of cloth increases. Thus, the quantity of imports demanded increases as the price ratio declines. (This is the downward-sloping demand-for-imports curve from Chapter 2.) As the relative price of cloth, the import good, declines (equivalently, as the relative price of wheat, the export good, increases), the country's terms of trade improve. As the relative price of cloth declines, the country reaches higher community indifference curves, so the country's well-being or welfare is increasing.

8. a.   Moonited Republic has an absolute advantage in wine—it takes fewer labor hours to produce a bottle (10<15). Moonited Republic also has an absolute advantage in producing cheese—it takes fewer labor hours to produce a kilo (4<10).

   b.   Moonited Republic has a comparative advantage in cheese—its relative advantage is largest in cheese ((4/10)<(10/15)). Vintland has a comparative advantage in wine—its relative disadvantage is smaller in wine ((15/10)<(10/4)). With no trade the relative price of cheese is 2/3 (=10/15) bottles of wine per kilo of cheese in Vintland, and it is 2/5 (=4/10) in Moonited Republic. Cheese is relatively cheap in Moonited Republic.

   c.

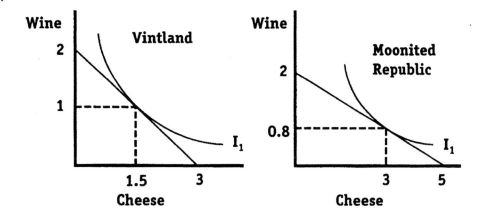

   d.   When trade is opened, Moonited Republic exports cheese and Vintland exports wine. If the equilibrium free trade price ratio is 1/2 bottle per kilo, Moonited Republic will specialize completely in producing cheese, and Vintland will specialize completely in producing wine.

e. With free trade Moonited Republic produces 5 (=20/4) million kilos of cheese. If it exports 2 million kilos, then it consumes 3 million kilos. It consumes the 1 million bottles of wine that it imports. With free trade Vintland produces 2 (=30/15) million bottles of wine. If it exports 1 million bottles, then it consumes 1 million bottles. It consumes the 2 million kilos of cheese that it imports.

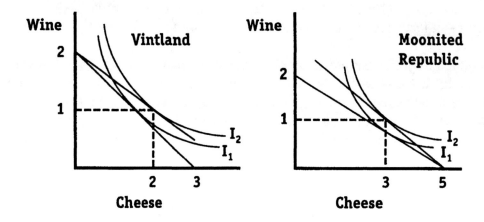

f. Each country gains from trade. Each is able to consume combined quantities of wine and cheese that are beyond its ability to produce domestically. (The free trade consumption point is outside of the production possibility curve.). Each reaches a better community indifference curve (I_2 rather than I_1 in each country).

10. If the number of labor hours to make a bushel of wheat is reduced by half to 1 hour, this reinforces the U.S. comparative advantage in wheat. (In fact, the United States then has an absolute advantage in wheat.) The United States is still predicted to export wheat and import cloth. If, instead, the number of hours to make a yard of cloth is reduced by half to 2 hours, this reduces the U.S. absolute disadvantage in cloth, but it does not change the pattern of comparative advantage. The relative price of cloth is now 1 (=2/2) bushel per yard in the United States with no trade, but this is still higher than the price of 0.67 bushel per yard in the rest of the world. The United States still has a comparative advantage in wheat, so the United States is still predicted to export wheat and import cloth.

12. a. Production remains at S_0, and the country can trade with the rest of the world at a price ratio of one bushel per yard. The country's consumption shifts to point $C_{0.5}$, and the country reaches community indifference curve $I_{1.5}$. The country gains from trade—its consumption point is outside of its production capabilities and it reaches a higher community indifference curve.

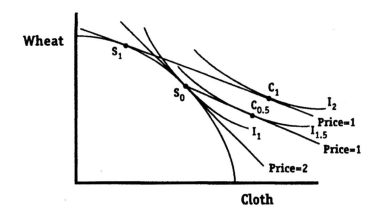

b. If the country adjusts its production point to the tangency at point S_1, it can consume at point C_1 and reach an even higher indifference curve I_1.

c. The trade volume grows. This is easiest to see for cloth imports. The quantity consumed of cloth increases and the quantity produced of cloth decreases, so the quantity imported of cloth increases. Because trade is balanced in both cases and the price ratio is the same (1 bushel per yard), the volume of wheat exports also increases.

15

Chapter 4

Who Gains and Who Loses from Trade?

Overview

This chapter has two major purposes. First, it examines the implications for factor income of trade that follows the Heckscher-Ohlin (H-O) theory. Second, it examines the empirical evidence on the Heckscher-Ohlin theory and some of its implications.

The implications of H-O trade for factor incomes follow from the pressures for changes in production levels as a country shifts from no trade to free trade. The export-oriented sector tries to expand production, as the relative price of the exportable good increases. The import-competing sector shrinks its production, as the relative price of the importable good decreases. In the short run, production factors cannot move easily between sectors. Therefore, in the short run, many or all factors employed in the export industry benefit from strong demand for their services and gain income. In the short run, many or all factors employed in the import-competing industry suffer from reduced demand for their services and lose income.

In the long run, the period of time that is emphasized by the Heckscher-Ohlin approach, factors can easily move between sectors. The implications for factor incomes then depends on the factors demanded by the expanding sector relative to the factors released by the contracting industry. According to the H-O theory, the expanding sector is intensive in the country's abundant factor, while the shrinking sector is intensive in the country's scarce factor. In the shift to free trade, there is strong demand for the abundant factor (relative to the small amount released as the import-competing sector shrinks), and there is weak demand for the scarce factor (relative to the large amount released as the import-competing sector shrinks.)   The shift to free trade increases the price and income of the abundant factor, and it decreases the price and income of the scarce factor. (The box "A Factor-Ratio Paradox" is difficult for some students, but it does show how full employment can be reached after the shift, as each sector alters the proportions in which it uses factors in response to the change in factor prices.)

Generally, the H-O approach has three major implications for factor incomes. First, the conclusion about the effect of opening to free trade is an example of the more general Stolper-Samuelson theorem—the real returns to the factor used intensively in a rising-price industry increase, and the real returns to the factor used intensively in the falling-price industry decline. This theorem applies in a number of situations, if certain conditions apply (including that the country produces both products both before and after the price change, and that the menu of technologies available does not change).

Second, another way to view the broad pattern of the effects of shifting to free trade (or other shifts which change relative product prices) is through the specialized-factor pattern—factors more specialized in the production of exportable products (or rising-price products more generally) tend to gain income, and factors more specialized in the production of import-competing products (or falling-price products more generally) tend to lose income. This pattern applies to both the short and the long run, and especially applies to factors that can only be used in one industry (sector-specific factors).

Third, the H-O approach has a surprising implication for the earnings of a single factor in different countries. The factor price equalization theorem states that free trade that equalizes product prices between countries also equalizes the prices of individual factors between countries. The logic of this can be developed intuitively. With no trade, the price of a factor will be "high" in the country in which it is scarce, and "low" in the country in which it is abundant. The shift to free trade increases the factor's price in the abundant country and decreases its price in the scarce country. Under "ideal" conditions, the factor's prices (in real terms) become equal in different countries. In its impact on differences in factor prices, product trade can be a substitute for international movement of factors.

The chapter then shifts to examine empirical evidence on the Heckscher-Ohlin theory. The box "The Leontief Paradox" summarizes the early tests. The text emphasizes the kinds of information that we need to examine real-world trade patterns—factor endowments and trade patterns, along with knowledge of the factor proportions used in producing different products. It provides evidence on endowments for six factors—physical capital, highly skilled labor, medium-skilled labor, unskilled labor, arable land, and forest land, and it discusses endowments of other natural resources. The examination of the U.S. pattern of international trade suggests that some of its trade seems consistent with the H-O predictions, but some also does not seem consistent. In general, trade patterns for the United States and other countries match the H-O theory reasonably well but not perfectly.

According to the H-O approach and the Stolper-Samuelson theorem, the factors that gain from free trade are those that are used intensively in export-oriented production, while the factors that lose are those used intensively in import-competing production. The chapter presents evidence on the factor content of export and import-competing production in the United States and Canada, along with brief comments about other countries.

Finally, the chapter provides evidence on international factor price equalization. While it clearly does not hold perfectly, even if we define factors carefully, we do see tendencies toward factor price equalization. Most obviously, as countries in Asia have integrated themselves into world trade, real wages in these countries have increased rapidly and approach the real wages earned by comparably skilled workers in industrialized countries.

The box "U.S. Jobs and Foreign Trade" provides a survey of the effects of international trade that focuses on employment. While this is not the most valid way to examine the effects of trade (as noted at the end of the box), it is the way that much of the debate actually occurs politically. The box shows that even on these terms the net effects on jobs are not clear, because reducing imports also tends to reduce exports.

The chapter's summary pulls together the answers that have been developed in Chapters 2-4 to the four key questions about trade presented at the beginning of Chapter 2.

Tips

We deliberately choose to bring out the implications for factor incomes using intuition and verbal logic. Although this sometimes requires statements that are a bit vague (e.g., high or low factor prices), it seems to work well in guiding most students to appreciate the reasons for and meanings of the implications. For instructors that wish to do this more formally, Appendix B is a starting point that presents the basics of the more formal analysis using the Edgeworth-Bowley box diagram.

The theory of international trade can appear to be abstract. In the book we try to bring out its application to the real world, often using the example of the United States. You may want to consider an assignment like the one that Pugel (and others at New York University) have been using successfully. It asks students to apply the theory to another country. The accompanying two pages under the heading "Sample Assignment" shows a version of this assignment. In this case students worked in groups on the assignment, but they could also be asked to work individually. (In addition, each group also worked on a second assignment later in the course using the same country.) The assignment might be distributed about the time that you cover Chapter 4 in the course. However, as you can see, it does ask for the application of concepts like intraindustry trade that are not covered until Chapter 6, so the due date should probably be after this material is presented in class, if you use a comparable assignment.

Suggested answers to questions and problems

(in textbook)

2. Not correct. First, it is not clear what this statement means. The real wage is measured per unit of labor and the real rental rate is measured per unit of land. Because the units of labor and land are not comparable, it is not clear in what sense the real wage and real rental rate could be "equal." Second, the factor price equalization holds for each type of income <u>across countries</u>. It says that free trade leads to the same real wage rate for labor (of a given type or skill) in different countries. It also says that free trade leads to the same real rental rate (for a given type of land) in different countries.

4. First, you might point out that stopping trading would also eliminate exports, so that many jobs would be lost in exporting industries. It is not clear that there would be a net gain in jobs, and any net gain would likely be small. In addition, total employment in the whole economy is essentially a macroeconomic concern that is best addressed through macroeconomic policies (the topic of Part IV of this book). Second, national well-being is much more than jobs. If we ended all trade, we would be giving up the gains from trade. Trade allows the country to sell some of its production as exports. These exports are used to pay for imports. Imports allow us to expand our consumption by giving us access to low-priced goods (and to goods that we cannot or do not produce domestically).

6. A decrease in the relative price of wheat leads to a decrease in domestic production of wheat. This is also an increase in the relative price of cloth, so there is an increase in the production of cloth. In the short run factors are mainly tied to their initial industries,

because there is limited mobility between industries. With a lower price of wheat and lower production, there is less demand for land and labor in the wheat industry, and both land and labor initially employed in the wheat industry tend to lose earnings (real income). With a higher price of cloth and efforts to expand cloth production, there is more demand for both land and labor in the cloth industry, and both land and labor initially employed in the cloth industry tend to gain earnings. In the long run, factors are mobile between industries. The shrinking of wheat production (assumed to be land-intensive) releases a relatively large amount of land and relatively little labor, while the expansion of the cloth industry requires a relatively large amount of labor and relatively little land. Thus, labor (throughout the economy) benefits from strong demand for its services, and the earnings of labor throughout the economy increase. Land (throughout the economy) experiences weak demand and the earnings of land decreases. The Stolper-Samuelson theorem predicts these long-run effects. A decrease in the relative price of wheat leads to a decrease in the real rental rate of land (the factor intensive in the decreasing-price industry) and an increase in the real wage of labor (the factor intensive in the other, rising-price industry).

8. a. If all factors are immobile, the increase in the relative price of wheat and the effort to expand wheat production tends to benefit the earnings of all factors initially employed in wheat production. This is also a decrease in the relative price of cloth, so that cloth production tends to decrease. This means that all factors initially employed in the cloth industry tend to lose earnings.

   b. If all factors are freely mobile between the wheat and cloth industries, the winners and losers depend on the increased demand for each factor as wheat production expands, relative to the release of each factor as cloth production decreases. The labor-intensity of the two industries is almost the same ($0.60 of labor use per dollar of wheat output and $0.59 per dollar of cloth output). The overall demand for labor is affected only a little as cloth shrinks and wheat expands, because the release of labor by cloth closely matches the need for additional labor in wheat. Labor throughout the economy is likely to be affected only a little by the change. Wheat is relatively land-intensive. The extra demand for land as wheat expands, relative to the smaller amount released as cloth shrinks, leads to an increase in the real return to land. Cloth is capital-intensive. The release of capital as cloth shrinks, relative to the smaller amount demanded as wheat expands, leads to a decrease in the real return to capital.

10. According to Figure 4.3, Japan is relatively abundant in physical capital, highly-skilled labor, and medium-skilled labor. Japan is relatively scarce in unskilled labor and arable and forest land. Japan is also relatively scarce in natural resources generally. (1) The following appear to be consistent with the predictions of the Heckscher-Ohlin theory. Japan is a substantial net importer of food (land-intensive), metal ores and petroleum and petroleum products (natural resource-intensive), and clothing and accessories and shoes and other footwear (unskilled labor-intensive). Japan is a substantial net exporter of iron and steel (physical capital-intensive) and computers and precision instruments (skilled labor-intensive). Substantial net exports of motor vehicles also appear to be consistent with the Heckscher-Ohlin theory, to the extent that their production is relatively physical capital-intensive (or skilled labor-intensive). (2) The following appear to inconsistent.

The relatively large amount of imports of chemicals (only a little less than Japanese exports of chemicals) appears to be inconsistent with the Heckscher-Ohlin theory, as chemical production is generally physical capital-intensive and skilled labor-intensive. The substantial net imports of aircraft also appear to inconsistent, as production of aircraft is intensive in skilled labor.

Sample assignment

NEW YORK UNIVERSITY
Stern School of Business

C45.0001 Economics of International Business
Prof. T. Pugel
Spring 1999

Country Assignment #1

This group assignment is due on Monday, March 8, 1999. NO LATE PAPERS WILL BE ACCEPTED.

The text of your group's answers to the assignment should be typed single-spaced, with an extra space between each paragraph. The text must be limited to a maximum of three pages. You may also attach additional tables and charts to this three pages of text, if these tables and charts are of direct importance to your answers.

The group members are not to discuss this assignment with anyone else who is not in the group (except for consulting reference librarians in order to locate materials). The group may utilize any published materials—you are not limited to the sources noted in the assignment description below.

Each group must choose one country that will be used for both this assignment and the second country assignment. For several different reasons, the country chosen cannot be any of the following: the United States, Germany, France, Italy, Austria, Belgium, Finland, Ireland, Luxembourg, Netherlands, Portugal, Spain, Japan, Canada, Singapore. Also, the country chosen cannot be a country which is the country of citizenship of any group member or a country in which any group member has lived for a period of one year or more.

Before your group commits to a choice of country, you might want to check to make sure that data are available for that country. Most importantly, you might want to check to make sure that the country chosen has useful data not only in the sources shown in the assignment below, but also in a publication of the International Monetary Fund—International Financial Statistics—that may be a major source for the second country assignment. Some countries are not shown in the UN and IMF books—for these countries, one must use other data sources (e.g., national reports), and this may be challenging. One final note on selecting a country—for the second country assignment, analysis of a country that has experienced very high inflation rates for part or all of the time since 1980 will be very interesting, but gathering and interpreting the data may be challenging.

The Assignment

1. For the most recent year for which data are available in the UN Yearbook noted below, present a full set of data (in easily readable form) on the country's exports and imports, at the two-digit SITC level. Which products are the country's major export products? Which

products are the country's major import products? (The text discussion for this part of the assignment should be brief and descriptive. It serves as an introduction to the rest of the report.)

Most likely data source: United Nations, <u>Yearbook of International Trade Statistics, 1996</u>. The SITC is the Standard International Trade Classification. Note: You should consult the notes at the beginning of the volume for information on such issues as SITC categories not reported in a particular table, and higher-digit SITC categories (e.g. 3-digit) that are equal to lower-digit SITC categories (e.g. 2-digit).

2. To what extent do various theories of trade appear to explain the country's commodity (product) pattern of trade (or to explain various aspects of this pattern)? In your answer here, you might examine the commodity pattern of exports, the commodity pattern of imports, the commodity pattern of net exports (exports minus imports) in absolute (money) amounts, and/or the commodity pattern of net exports of each product as a percentage of total trade (exports plus imports) of this product by the country. In addition, the extent of intraindustry trade in the various products should also be documented and examined with reference to theory.

3. For the most recent year for which data are available, document the five countries that are the largest buyers of your country's exports. For the most recent year for which data are available, document the five countries that are the largest sources of your country's imports. Discuss briefly the probable reasons for this pattern of major trading-partner countries. (Your discussion may need to incorporate reasons that go beyond what we have discussed in class.)

Most likely data source: International Monetary Fund, <u>Direction of Trade Statistics Yearbook.</u>

Chapter 5

Growth and Trade

Overview

This chapter has two major purposes. First, it shows how the Heckscher-Ohlin model can be used to analyze economic growth and its impact on international trade. Second, it examines additional aspects of technological progress and its relationship to international trade.

Growth in a country's production capabilities shifts the country's production possibilities curve out. Growth is balanced if the ppc shifts out proportionately. Balanced growth could occur because all factors are growing at similar rates, or because production technology is improving at the same rate in both sectors. Growth is biased if the outward shift in the ppc is skewed, so that the growth favors producing more of one product than the other. Biased growth could occur if one factor is growing more quickly than the other, or if production technology is improving more in one sector than the other. (For instance, if only one product's production technology is improving, then the ppc intercept with the other product's axis does not change—see footnote 1 in the text.)

One example of very biased growth is growth in only one factor, the other factor unchanged. While the entire ppc shifts out, the growth is strongly biased in favor of the product that uses the growing factor intensively. The Rybczynski theorem indicates that, if product prices are constant, then the output quantity of the product that uses the growing factor intensively will increase, while the output quantity of the other product must contract. The reason is that expanding production of the intensive good also requires some of the other factor. This amount of the other factor must be drawn from the other industry, so its output declines. A box applies this concept to the "Dutch disease" of deindustrialization following discovery and development of production of a natural resource.

The growth of the country's production capabilities is likely to change the country's willingness to trade—the quantities that it wants to export and import—even if product prices do not change. The change in the country's willingness can be documented by examining the change in the country's trade triangle for the price ratio that held in the free-trade equilibrium before the growth occurs. The change in the production point depends on whether growth is balanced or biased. The change in the consumption point depends on tastes in the country. At the same price ratio the quantities consumed of both products will increase if both goods are normal. Growth that is balanced or biased toward producing the exportable product is likely to increase the country's willingness to trade. Growth that is sufficiently biased toward producing more of the importable product will reduce the country's willingness to trade.

If the country is small, then changes in its trade have essentially no impact on the world equilibrium price ratio. In this case the analysis just presented using the initial price ratio is the complete picture.

If instead this is a large country, then changes in its willingness to trade change the equilibrium international price ratio. If the growth reduces the country's willingness to trade, then the reduced supply of exports and the reduced demand for imports results in an increase in the equilibrium relative price of the country's exportable product. The well-being of the country increases for two reasons—the country's production capabilities increase, and its terms of trade improve.

If growth increases the willingness to trade of a large country, then the increased supply of exports and the increased demand for imports results in a decrease in the equilibrium relative price of the country's exportable product. If the price does not change by too much, then the country's well-being is higher—but the increase in well-being is less than it would be if the country's terms of trade did not deteriorate. If the price ratio changes by a lot then immiserizing growth is possible—growth that expands the country's willingness to trade causes such a large decline in the country's terms of trade that the well-being of the country declines. The loss from the decline in the terms of trade is larger than the gain from the larger production capabilities. This is more likely if the growth is strongly biased toward producing more of the exportable product, foreign demand for the country's exports is price inelastic, and the country is heavily engaged in international trade.

The discussion of technology and trade focuses on several main points. First, differences in production technologies available in different countries can be the source of comparative advantage, because technology differences result in production possibility curves that are skewed differently in different countries. Second, much new technology is the result of organized research and development (R&D). The location of the production of new technology through R&D follows the Heckscher-Ohlin theory. R&D is intensive in the use of highly skilled labor (especially scientists and engineers) and also in capital that is willing to take large risks (for instance, venture capital). Consistent with H-O theory, most new technology is created by R&D located in the industrialized countries, which are well-endowed with these factors. Third, although production using the new technology may first occur in the country that creates the new technology, the technology is also likely to diffuse internationally. The product cycle hypothesis suggest that there is a regular pattern as new technology diffuses, with developing countries often becoming the exporters of many products after the products become standardized or mature. Although the product cycle describes the evolution of production and trade for a number of products, it is also subject to a number of limitations.

Openness to international trade can also increase a country's growth rate. Imports can speed diffusion of new production technology into a country, through imports of advanced capital goods and, more generally, through greater awareness of new foreign technology. Openness to trade can also place additional competitive pressure on domestic firms to develop and adopt new technology, and export sales can increase the returns to their R&D activities. According to the "new growth theory," these increases in the country's current technology base can enhance ongoing innovation, resulting in a higher ongoing growth rate.

Finally, the box "Trade, Technology, and U.S. Wages" confronts an important issue—why has the difference in wages between skilled and less skilled workers been widening since the 1970s, in the United States and other countries. This could be the Stolper-Samuelson theorem at work, if expanding trade with developing countries placed downward pressure on the prices of products intensive in less skilled labor. But several studies conclude that this effect is smaller than another—biases in technological change. Technological change seems to have created rising demand for skilled labor for two reasons. First, technological progress has been faster in industries that are intensive in skilled labor, resulting in their faster growth. Second, technological progress is biased in favor of using more skilled labor.

Tips

This chapter is written to take the reader through the analysis of growth step-by-step—the change in the production possibility curve, the change in the willingness to trade, the change in the international equilibrium price ratio, and the overall effects of growth on the country, including both the production growth and the change in the country's terms of trade. It provides a major application of the key tools from Chapter 3—the production possibility curve, the community indifference curves, and trade triangles. It attempts to cover the range of major cases that can arise, without becoming overly taxonomic.

In class presentation of this material, we have found that it is useful for the instructor, after briefly summarizing the generic process of the analysis, to present the entire analysis of each of several specific examples. For instance, the example of growth of the scarce factor of production can be used to introduce the Rybczynski theorem and to bring out the terms-of-trade effects of growth that reduces a large country's willingness to trade. The example can include discussion of comparison of the country's well-being and its production and consumption points before the growth and after the growth (inclusive of the change in the price ratio). In addition, the implication for factor incomes can be noted by referring back to the general Stolper-Samuelson theorem. It is also possible to draw out the implications for the other (the non-growing) country. Then, a second example can be examined from start to finish, such as technological improvement only in the country's export sector (with no diffusion to the other country). This example can be used to bring out the terms-of-trade effects of growth that increases a large country's willingness to trade, and this can lead into a discussion of the possibility of immiserizing growth.

Suggested answers to questions and problems
(in the textbook)

2. Disagree. According to the Rybczynski theorem, an increase in the country's labor force will result in an increase in the quantity produced of the labor-intensive good, and a decrease in the quantity produced of the other good. The additional labor goes to work in the labor-intensive industry. But, to expand production of this good, extra non-labor resources (e.g., land) are needed to work with the extra labor. These extra non-labor resources are drawn from the other industry, so production of the other good decreases.

4. Disagree. Immiserizing growth can occur if growth in the country leads the country to want to trade more, and the country's terms of trade deteriorate by a large amount. If a

country's trade has almost no impact on world prices, then its growth will have almost no impact on its terms of trade, and immiserizing growth is very unlikely.

6. According to the product life cycle approach, the technological originator of a product eventually will import the product. But its overall trade need not develop into chronic "deficits." As the technological originator continues to develop new products, it will export these products, while importing older products.

8. a. This can lead to a reversal of the trade pattern. If the initially scarce factor grows by enough, then it will become the relatively abundant factor in the country, and Heckscher-Ohlin theory predicts that the trade pattern will reverse.

   b. This can lead to a reversal of the trade pattern. If a country initially exported a product because it had a technological advantage in that product, then diffusion of the technology to other countries could result in these other countries' becoming the low-cost producers, so the first country becomes an importer of the product. This pattern is stressed in the product cycle approach.

   c. This can lead to a reversal of the trade pattern. Consider a country that initially exports wheat. If local consumers shift their tastes strongly toward consuming more wheat, they may demand so much wheat that none is left for export, and some amount of imports may be needed to satisfy the increased domestic demand.

10. a. Typically we expect that the drought in East Asia would result in East Asia demanding more imports of food, so East Asia becomes more willing to trade.

    b. The increase in East Asian demand for imports of food (or, equivalently, the decrease in world supply of food) results in an increase in the equilibrium relative price of food.

    c. In the United States, there is no drought and no change in the U.S. production possibility curve. The increase in the relative price of food (decrease in the relative price of clothing) causes production to shift from S_1 to S_2, more food produced and less clothing produced domestically. Given the new production point S_2, the United States can trade at the new price ratio to reach consumption point C_2. In comparison with initial consumption at C_1, the United States has higher well-being or welfare, reaching community indifference I_2 rather than I_1. (The higher welfare is the result of the improved terms of trade.) The relative price of clothing decreases and U.S. real income increases, so the quantity consumed of clothing increases. Quantity consumed of food could increase, stay the same, or decrease. The United States tends to consume more food because U.S. real income has increased. The United States tends to consume less food because the relative price of food has increased. The actual change in the quantity of food consumed depends on the relative sizes of these two effects—the income and substitution effects.

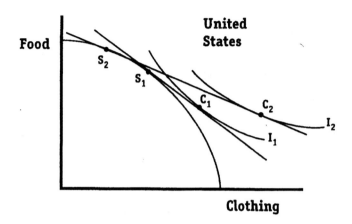

d.   According to the Stolper-Samuelson theorem, the factor (land) used intensively in food production (the rising-price good) gains real income. The factor (labor) used intensively in producing clothing (the falling-price good) loses real income.

12. a.   For the rest of the world, the production possibility curve does not change, but the equilibrium relative price of clothing declines. Production in the rest of the world shifts from, say, point S_1 to point S'. Clothing production declines and food production increases in the rest of the world. The rest of the world can trade at the new price ratio, and its consumption point shifts from point C_1 to point C'. The rest of the world shifts from I_1 to I', a lower community indifference curve, so its well-being or welfare declines. The relative price of food increases and real income is lower in the rest of the world, so its quantity consumed of food decreases. The quantity consumed of clothing can decrease, stay the same, or increase. Real income is lower, which tends to lower quantity consumed of clothing. The relative price of clothing is lower, which tends to increase the quantity consumed of clothing. The actual change depends on which of these two effects is larger.

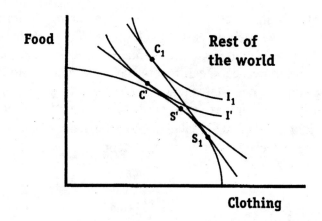

b.   Well-being or welfare in the rest of the world decreases because its terms of trade deteriorate. The price that it gets for its exports of clothing decreases. The purchasing power of its exports decreases, so the country can afford to buy fewer imports, and the country is poorer.

Chapter 6

Alternative Theories of Trade

Overview

This chapter surveys several theories of international trade that are alternatives to the standard theory based on perfectly competitive markets with constant or increasing costs. These alternative theories are based on some form of increasing returns to scale, so that unit costs tend to decline as output increases.

Several trade facts indicate the need for alternative theories. First, much trade, especially trade in manufactured goods among industrialized countries, is intra-industry trade—two-way trade in the same or very similar goods. Second, some industries are global oligopolies—a few firms account for most of global sales.

While there may be a number of explanations of intra-industry trade, product differentiation seems to be the major one. The market structure of monopolistic competition is useful for analyzing the role of product differentiation. Each producer faces a downward-sloping demand curve for its product variety. If scale economies (internal to the firm) are moderate (relative to the size of the total market for all varieties of this product), then free entry drives each firm to earn a normal profit (the average cost curve is tangent to the demand curve). If a monopolistically competitive market is opened to international trade, then a domestic consumer has access to additional varieties of the product—those that can be imported. A domestic producer has access to additional buyers—foreigners who prefer its variety. Product differentiation in this monopolistically competitive global market is the basis for intra-industry, as some varieties are imported while others are exported.

With this kind of trade, an additional source of gains from trade for the country is the increase in varieties that become available. Furthermore, trade may also lead to lower prices for the domestic varieties. These benefits accrue to consumers generally. The implications of trade for the well-being of different groups in the country are also modified. First, if most trade is intra-industry, then there may be little pressure on factor prices caused by inter-industry shifts in factor demand. Second, the gains from increased varieties reduce the loss to factors that suffer income losses due to Stolper-Samuelson effects. Some may believe they are better off even though they appear to lose income.

In some industries, a few large firms account for most global sales, perhaps because internal scale economies are large. In such an oligopoly each firm should recognize interdependence with the other large firms—its actions and decisions are likely to elicit responses from the other firms. Competition then resembles a game, but it is still not clear how the firms should play the game. If they compete aggressively, then they may earn only normal profits. If instead they restrain their competitive thrusts, then they may be able to earn high profits. However, they may be caught in the prisoners dilemma of competing aggressively, unless they can find some way to cooperate.

Although we do not have a full theory of oligopoly, we can make several observations about oligopoly and trade. First, scale economies tend to concentrate production in a few production sites. When they were chosen by the firms, these may have been the lowest-cost sites. Over time production tends to continue in these sites, even though they may not remain the lowest cost sites if all sites could achieve the same production scale. Second, the fact that oligopoly firms can earn high profits means that it matters where these firms are located (or who owns them). The high profits earned on export sales creates another source of national gains from trade (in the form of better terms of trade, and at the expense of foreign buyers).

A third alternative theory is based on scale economies that are external to the individual firm but arise from advantages of having a high level of production in a geographic area. With external economies an expansion of demand (such as that caused by increased exports) can result in a lower unit cost for all producers in the area and a lower product price. With free trade production tends to be concentrated in one or a few locations. In the shift from no trade to free trade, production in some locations would increase so that their unit costs and prices fell, while production in other locations would decrease or cease. It is not easy to predict which locations become dominant—history, luck, or government policy may be important. The importing countries gain from trade, even if local production ceases, because consumers benefit from the lower prices of the imported product. A key difference from the standard model is that with external scale economies consumers in the exporting country also gain surplus as trade leads to lower costs and prices, because production is concentrated in few locations that can better achieve the external economies.

The chapter concludes with a summary that pulls together the sweep of the analysis of international trade covered in Part I (Chapters 2-6).

Tips

The table shown with Chapter 2 of this Manual could instead be introduced as a summary device at the conclusion of the classroom presentation of the material in Chapter 6.

The link of global oligopoly to trade policy—often called strategic trade policy—is presented in Chapter 10.

The country assignment included as a Suggested Assignment for Chapter 4 includes a question referring to the country's intra-industry trade. If appropriate, you could ask a more specific question, which might include calculation of the intra-industry trade share using the formula in the text.

Suggested answers to questions and problems
(in textbook)

2. Economies of scale exist when unit (or average) cost declines as production during a period of time is larger. (1) The key role of economies of scale in the analysis of markets that are monopolistically competitive is to provide an incentive for larger production levels of each variety of the industry's product. The product is differentiated, but it is not fully customized to each individual consumer's exact desires. Larger production runs of each variety of the product can benefit from economies of scale. Still, these scale economies apply mainly to relatively small levels of production, so that a large number of firms and product varieties can exist and compete in the market. (2) The key role of economies of scale in the analysis of oligopoly is that they drive firms to become large, so that a small number of firms come to dominate the market. These scale economies apply over a large range of output, so that firms that are large relative to the size of the market enjoy cost advantages over any smaller rivals.

4. If the government is going to permit free export of the pasta (no export taxes or export limits), then the government should choose to form the industry as a monopoly. The country is likely to gain more from trade if it charges a higher price to foreign buyers, because the country benefits from higher export prices and better terms of trade. A monopoly will charge higher prices (in order to maximize its profits), in comparison with the equilibrium price for a comparable but competitive industry. Because all of the product is exported, there is no concern with charging domestic consumers high prices. The goal is to charge foreign buyers high prices. The gains from better terms of trade accrue mainly to the monopoly as higher profits. This benefits the country as long as the monopoly is owned by the country's residents (or the country's government can gain some of these profits through taxation).

6. a. The market equilibrium price depends on how intensely Boeing and Airbus compete in order to gain sales. A low-price equilibrium occurs if Boeing and Airbus compete intensely to gain extra sales, including attempts to use price-cutting to "steal" sales from each other. A high-price equilibrium occurs if Boeing and Airbus recognize that price competition mainly serves to depress the profits of both firms, so that they both restrain their urges to compete using low prices.

   b. From the perspective of the well-being or welfare of the United States or Europe, a high-price equilibrium could be desirable because it involves setting high prices on export sales to other countries. This equilibrium results in sales to domestic buyers at high prices, so there is some loss of pricing efficiency domestically. But the benefits to the country from charging high prices on exports and improving its terms of trade can easily be larger, so that overall the high-price equilibrium can be desirable.

   c. The low-price outcome is desirable for a country like Japan or Brazil that imports all of its large passenger jet airplanes (e.g., for use by its national airlines). The country's terms of trade are better if import prices are lower.

   d. Yes, Japan or Brazil still gains from importing airplanes. Some amount of "consumer surplus" is obtained by these countries—that is why they import even at the high price. But their surplus would be even greater if airplane prices were low.

8. a. Using the formula from the text, the IIT share for the United States equals 1 - (18.9 + 19.4 + 7.5 + 34.9 + 12.2 + 9.4 + 12.3 + 53.4)/(101.5 + 31.8 + 31.3 + 48.3 + 12.2 + 21.8 +

31

58.5 + 151.8) = 1 - 168.0/457.2 = 0.63. For these products 63 percent of U.S. trade is intra-industry trade.

b.   Using the same approach, the IIT share for Japan for these products equals 1 - 65/157 = 0.59. For these products 59 percent of Japan's trade is intra-industry trade.

c.   For these products the United States engages in somewhat more intra-industry trade. Other, more comprehensive studies reach the same conclusion, and they usually find that the difference is larger.

10. a.   Among the strong arguments are the following. First, freer trade brings gains from trade, even for products that can be produced locally. With freer trade resources can be reallocated to producing exports. These exports can be used to buy imports at a cost that is lower than the cost of producing these products domestically. Because of relatively cheap imports, the country's total consumption can exceed its abilities to produce domestically. Second, some products are not produced domestically but can be imported. The country gains because consumers have access to a wider variety of products. Third, import competition provides competitive discipline for domestic monopolies and oligopolies. Prices will be driven closer to marginal costs, so that the efficiency of the market is enhanced. Fourth, access to imports and import competition will spur technological progress. Industries that are sheltered from international competition may lack the spur to improve technology; indeed, they may even lack the knowledge of technological progress that is occurring elsewhere in the world. Freer trade creates the competitive spur to improve technologies and increases the likelihood that information on new technologies will diffuse into the economy.

b.   With respect to short-run pressures on economic well-being, owners of factors employed in industries that could expand exports are likely to support the policy shift, because the demand for these factors increases as firms attempt to expand production. Owners of factors employed in industries that will receive increased competition from imports are likely to oppose the policy shift (unless they feel that other benefits from such changes as greater product variety and better overall technology more than offset their direct income losses). With respect to long-run pressures on economic well-being, the Stolper-Samuelson theorem is relevant. Owners of India's abundant factors of production are likely to support the policy shift, because they will gain real income. Owners of India's scarce factors are likely to oppose the shift, because they will lose real income (again, unless other benefits more than offset the direct income loss).

Chapter 7

The Basic Analysis of a Tariff

Overview

This chapter begins the analysis of government policies that limit imports, by examining the tariff—a government tax on imports. The chapter has two major purposes. First, the analysis shows the effects of a tariff when the importing country is small, so that its import policies have no effect on world prices. Second, the analysis of a large importing country—one whose policies can affect world prices—shows that a large country can use a tariff to lower the price that it pays foreigners for its imports.

We begin by examining the effects of a tariff imposed by a small country (contrasted with free trade), using supply and demand within the importing country. Since foreign exporters do not change the price that they charge for the product, the domestic price of the imported product rises by the amount of the tariff. Domestic producers competing with these imports can also raise their domestic prices as the domestic price of imports rises. Domestic producers gain when the government imposes a tariff on competing imports. They get a higher price for their products, they produce and sell a larger quantity (a movement along the domestic supply curve), and they receive more producer surplus. (The effects of the entire tariff system on domestic producers can be more complicated than this, because other tariffs can raise the costs of materials and components. The box on "The Effective Rate of Protection" discusses this more complete analysis, focusing on the effects of the tariff system on value added per unit of domestic production.)

Domestic consumers of the product are also affected by the imposition of the tariff. They must pay a higher price (for both imported and domestically produced products), they reduce the quantity that they buy and consume (a movement along the domestic demand curve), and they suffer a loss of consumer surplus.

The government also collects tariff revenue, equal to the tariff rate per unit imported times the quantity that is imported with the tariff is imposed (less than the free-trade import quantity).

We thus have two domestic winners (domestic producers and the national government) and one domestic loser (domestic consumers) because of the imposition of a tariff. We can evaluate the net effect on the whole country, if we have some way of comparing winners and losers. As we did beginning in Chapter 2, we can, for instance, use the one-dollar-one-vote measure. Part of what consumers lose is matched by the gain to domestic producers, and another part is matched by the revenue gain to the government. But there is an additional amount that consumers lose and that is not a gain to the other groups. This is the net national loss from a tariff (for a small country). In the national market graph this loss is two triangles; equivalently, in the import-export graph this loss is one triangle.

If we look at the national market graph, we can see why these are deadweight losses. The consumption effect of the tariff is the loss of consumer surplus for those consumers who are squeezed out of the market because the tariff "artificially" raises the domestic price, even though foreigners remain willing to sell products to the importing country at the lower world price. The production effect of the tariff is the loss from using high-cost domestic production to replace lower-cost imports (available to the country at the unchanged world price). The high production cost is shown by the height of the supply curve, for each of the extra units produced because of the tariff.

The analysis is affected in important ways if the importing country is a large country, one that has monopsony power in world markets. A large country can gain from the terms-of-trade effect when it imposes a tariff. The tariff reduces the amount that the country wants to import, so foreign exporters lower their price (a movement along the foreign supply-of-exports curve). We analyze the large country case using the international market (imports and exports), and we show the tariff as driving a wedge between demand and supply, so the price to the import buyers exceeds the price received by foreign exporters by the amount of the tariff. For the large importing country, the imposition of the tariff causes a triangle of national loss (comparable to the one shown for the small country) but also a rectangle of national gain because the price paid to foreign exporters is lowered, for the units that the country continues to import.

The net effect on the importing country depends on which of these two is larger. For a suitably small tariff, the rectangle is larger, so the importing country has a net gain from imposing a tariff. A prohibitive tariff would cause a net national loss, because the rectangle would disappear. It is possible to determine the country's optimal tariff—the tariff rate that makes the net gain to the importing country as large as possible. The optimal tariff rate is inversely related to the price elasticity of foreign supply of the country's imports.

We conclude by pointing out that the optimal tariff causes a net loss to the whole world. The loss to the foreign exporting country is larger than the net gain to the importing country. And a country trying to impose an optimal tariff risks retaliation by the foreign countries hurt by the country's tariff.

Tips

This chapter is crucial to understanding the effects of government policies toward trade. We recommend a strategy of "stereo" coverage. Every key point should be expressed in written words as well as in diagrams, in lecture as well as in the textbook.

A requirement for clear understanding throughout Part II is that students know how to interpret the height of the demand curve as marginal benefits and the height of the supply curve as marginal costs, leading them to measures of consumer surplus and producer surplus. If students have not mastered these concepts in other courses, they must be taken through this material in

Chapter 2. Even a course that wants to go quickly to government policies toward trade, skipping the details of trade theory, should start with Chapter 2.

In the textbook, we choose to show the optimal tariff using only demand-for-imports and supply-of-exports in the international market. In class session you may want to show the analysis in the equivalent way, using the national market. This can be useful to show the full range of effects when a large country imposes a tariff: increase in domestic producer surplus; decrease in domestic consumer surplus; government tariff revenue, with some of it paid by domestic consumers and some effectively paid by foreign exporters, compared with the free-trade price; and the net effect on national well-being as the difference between the rectangle of gain from the lower price paid to foreign exporters and the two triangles of loss.

We present the analysis of a tariff in this chapter for both the small country and the large country, and we present the analysis of an import quota and a voluntary export restraint (VER) in the next chapter. In your class presentation you might consider a different way of organizing this material, in which you present the small country analysis of the tariff, the quota, and the VER as a package, and then turn to looking at the large country analysis of the tariff and the quota. This alternative approach is designed to emphasize the fundamental similarities of the analyses of these different government policies, as well as the specific ways in which they are different. Students generally find it easier to grasp the small country analyses, so it can be useful to do all three policies for this easier case before turning to the large country analyses.

For those who want to present a more technical analysis of the optimal tariff, the first section of Appendix D presents the basic mathematics. The third section of Appendix D shows how to use offer curves and trade indifference curves to determine the optimal tariff.

Suggested answers to questions and problems

(in the textbook)

2.   Agree. The tariff raises the domestic price of the imported product, and domestic producers of the product raise their price when the domestic price of imports increases. Domestic consumers lose consumer surplus on the total amount that they consume, both imports and domestically produced product, because of the increase in domestic price. Domestic producers gain producer surplus on the amount that they produce and sell, because of the increase in domestic price. Consumers lose more because the domestic quantity consumed is larger than the domestic quantity produced.

4.   The consumption effect of a tariff is the loss of consumer surplus for the units that consumers would consume with free trade but do not consume when the tariff increases the domestic price. The tariff "artificially" raises the domestic price and causes some consumers to buy less of the product. On a diagram like Figure 7.3 or 7.4A, it is the triangular area d.

6.   For a small country the world price of $400 will not be affected by the tariff. The size of the net national loss from imposing a $40 tariff will depend on the shapes of the domestic supply and demand curves. The graph shows several possible domestic supply and demand curves. (We will assume that supply and demand are straight lines.)

The maximum net national loss occurs when the two triangles of deadweight loss are as large as possible. The maximum loss occurs when the $40 tariff just eliminates all imports, so that the country shifts to no trade with a domestic price of $440. The tariff imposes a full $40 price distortion on the full amount of free-trade imports of 0.4 million per year. In the graph, any curves like S_1 and D_1, which have free-trade at A and B and intersect each other at a price of $440, will cause a net national loss shown by the shaded triangle. The size of the loss is $(½)·(1.4 - 1.0)·($40) = 8 million.

The minimum net national loss is zero. This can occur in any of several extreme cases. First, if both the supply curve and the demand curve are vertical (S_0 and D_0), then the domestic price increases to $440, but there are no changes of quantities. With no distortion of domestic producer and consumer decisions, there are no triangles of inefficiency. Second, if the domestic demand curve is flat (D_3), then domestic consumers receive no consumer surplus at the price of $400, and they will not pay more than $400 per bike. When the tariff is imposed, imports fall to zero, domestic price remains at $400, and domestic production remains at 1.0 million bikes. There are no triangles of loss. Third, if the domestic supply curve is flat (S_3), then domestic producers receive no producer surplus at the price of $400, and they can supply more bikes at the same price. When the tariff is imposed, imports fall to zero, domestic price remains at $400, and domestic production increases to match domestic consumption at 1.4 million bikes. There are no triangles of loss.

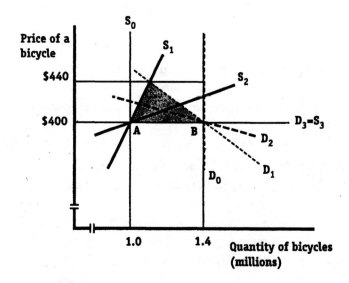

8.   If imports are 0.33 million bicycles, the tariff-inclusive price paid by domestic consumers must be $350, and the export price is $250, so the tariff is $100 per bicycle. The

36

importing country gains the rectangle equal to $50·0.33 million = $16.7 million. It loses the triangle equal to (½)·$50·0.67 = $16.7 million. The net national gain is zero.

10. The formula is $1/s_m$, where s_m is the foreign elasticity of export supply (foreign supply of our imports). If the foreign supply is infinitely elastic, then the optimal tariff is zero (= $1/\infty$).

Chapter 8

Nontariff Barriers to Imports

Overview

This chapter has four major purposes:
1. Introduce the World Trade Organization (WTO) and the General Agreement on Tariffs and Trade (GATT), as well as the result of the Uruguay Round of multilateral trade negotiations.
2. Present analysis of an import quota and a voluntary export restraint (VER), for both a small importing country and a large one.
3. Provide an overview of other nontariff barriers (NTBs) to imports.
4. Examine estimates of the costs of actual tariffs and nontariff barriers.

Created by the Uruguay Round trade agreement, the World Trade Organization, which incorporates the General Agreement on Tariffs and Trade, is the multilateral institution that oversees the global rules of government trade policies. Under the GATT, countries engaged in 8 rounds of trade negotiations that were successful in lowering the tariff rates of industrialized countries. The two most recent rounds also attempted to liberalize NTBs, but with less success. (The box on the Uruguay Round summarizes the major features of the wide-ranging agreements that came out of these negotiations.)

The chapter then turns to analysis of an import quota. If both the domestic industry and the foreign export industry are perfectly competitive, then the effects of a quota are almost all the same as the effects of a tariff that permits the quantity of imports. For a small importing country, the increase in domestic price, the increase in domestic production, the decrease in domestic consumption, the increase in domestic producer surplus, the decrease of domestic consumer surplus, and the net national loss are the same. The possible difference is what happens to the amount that would be government revenue with a tariff. With an import quota this is the amount that is the difference between the cost of imports purchased from foreign exporters at the world price and the value of these quota-limited imports when sold in the domestic market at the higher domestic price. (We presume that the holders of the import quota rights can continue to buy at the world price. If any foreign exporter tried to charge more, the importers would turn to other export suppliers who would sell at the going world price.)

If the government gives away these quota rights to import with no application procedure (fixed favoritism), then the import price markup goes as extra profits to whoever is lucky enough to receive the rights. If the government auctions the quota rights (import-license auction), then the government gains the markup as auction revenues because bidders vie for these valuable import rights. If the government uses elaborate applications procedures (resource-using application), then some of the markup amount is lost to resource usage in the application process, leading to a larger net national loss because of the extra resource costs of the quota process.

For the large-country case, again the effects of imposing a quota are nearly all the same as the equivalent tariff, except for what happens to what would be tariff revenue. Specifically, the importing country can benefit from imposing an import quota, if the rectangle of gain from the lower price paid to foreign exporters for the quota quantity imported is larger than the triangle losses from distorting domestic production and consumption.

If the domestic industry is a monopoly, then the effects of imposing a quota are different from the effects of imposing a tariff. The text of the chapter briefly explains that a quota cuts off foreign competition, so the monopoly-creating quota leads to a higher domestic price and greater national losses. Appendix E provides a more rigorous analysis of this case.

The VER is usually not voluntary, but it is an export restraint. Because the government of the exporting country must organize its exporters into a kind of cartel, they should realize that they should raise the export price. If the exporters do raise the export price, then the exporters get the amount that otherwise would be government revenue with a tariff, or the price markup with an import quota. The net national loss is larger for the importing country with a VER because of this additional rectangle loss.

Governments use a variety of other barriers to imports in addition to tariffs. NTBs lower imports by directly limiting the quantity of imports (e.g., import quota, VER, government procurement policies that prohibit or limit government purchasing of imports), increasing the costs of getting imports into the market (e.g., applications and testing procedures), and creating uncertainty about whether imports will be permitted (e.g., arbitrary licensing procedures). The chapter examines two NTBs, product standards and domestic content requirements. Product standards can be worthy efforts to protect health, safety, and the environment. But they can also be written to limit imports and protect domestic producers. Domestic content requirements limit the import of components and materials by requiring that a minimum percentage of the value of a product produced or sold in a country be local value added (wages and domestically produced components and materials).

Section 301 of the U.S. Trade Act of 1974 is an unusual government policy. Its goal is to lower foreign barriers to U.S. exports, including failure of foreign countries to protect intellectual property rights (patents, trademarks, copyrights, and trade secrets). But it tries to do this by threatening to raise U.S. barriers to the foreign country's exports if the foreign country does not change its policies. Other countries resent such a heavy-handed approach. And, if the U.S. government carries out the threat, then the approach backfires—it probably lowers well-being for both countries. Fortunately, the United States has decreased its use of Section 301. With the establishment of the WTO with its strong dispute settlement procedures, the United States is more likely to send its complaints about unfair foreign trade practices to the WTO for resolution.

How large are the effects of actual tariffs, quotas, VERs, and other nontariff barriers to imports? The chapter begins the answer by showing that the net national loss is probably a small fraction of the value of domestic production (GDP), for a country like the United States that has moderate import barriers and is not highly dependent on imports, if the only national losses are the deadweight-loss triangles. The true cost is probably larger than this basic analysis indicates, because of foreign retaliation and losses in export industries, the costs of enforcing import barriers, the costs of rent-seeking activities like lobbying for import protection, and losses from reduced pressures to innovate. In addition, the costs from raising barriers would accelerate in a nonlinear way, and the areas of the triangles would increase rapidly.

Another way to look at the size of the effects of protection is per dollar of increase in domestic producer surplus. Figure 8.3 shows the results of a study of 23 U.S. industries that receive substantial import protection. Each dollar of increase in producer surplus causes a net loss to the U.S. economy of $0.49 (the rest of the U.S. economy loses $1.49). The net world efficiency loss is $0.35 per dollar of gain to U.S. producer surplus.

Tips

Many of the tips for Chapter 7 also apply to this chapter. We strongly recommend showing the effects of quotas and VERs using both words and diagrams.

The material of Chapter 8 can be supplemented with outside readings on the WTO or news items on current trade policy issues. Students appreciate seeing how the concepts and analyses connect to real issues, and governments are usually accommodating in serving up fresh examples.

Suggested answers to questions and problems
(in the textbook)

2.   Voluntary export restraint (VER) agreements are nontariff barriers to imports. Despite their name, the importing-country government coerces the exporting-country government into allocating a limited quota of exports among its exporting firms. Import-country governments often force exporters into accepting VERs because the government wants to limit imports without explicit import barriers like tariffs or import quotas that would violate international agreements. (The Uruguay Round agreements include a provision to reduce and eliminate the use of VERs, but it remains to be seen if this will be effective.) In choosing VERs, the importing-country government does not create a bigger national gain than with tariffs or quotas. On the contrary, a VER allows foreign exporters to gain the full price markup that the importing country would have kept for itself if it had used a tariff or quota. (Gaining this price markup is a reason that the exporting country may agree to a VER, rather than risking that the importing-country government will impose its own import limits.)

4. a.   Product standards are imposed to assure that products meet minimum requirements to protect health, safety, or the environment. But they can be written to discriminate against imports, by setting unreasonable requirements that penalize imports. To the extent that product standards enhance health, safety, and the environment, they can raise national well-being. To the extent that they are used as nontariff barriers to imports, they bring the net national losses that usually accompany protection.

b. Domestic content requirements force producers to limit the use of imported components and materials by mandating that a minimum percentage of the value of a product be domestic value added (wages of local workers and domestically produced materials and components). This provides protection for domestic producers of materials and components and results in the net national losses that usually accompany protection.

6. a. The U.S. government is deeply committed to assuring that food products are safe for consumers to eat, and to protecting the health and safety of workers growing the food. These are surely noble and correct goals for government regulations. We have established regulations for growing and harvesting apples that assure that they meet these objectives. In particular, U.S. standards regulate the use of various pesticides and prohibit the use of unsafe pesticides, to protect worker health and to minimize or prevent ingestion by consumers of trace amounts of pesticides. The U.S. government must insist that U.S. production standards be followed in foreign countries for all apples exported to the United States. Otherwise the U.S. government could not be certain to meet its objectives for imported apples.

   b. The U.S. government has no business forcing us to adopt its production standards. First, our own governments are the best judges of the standards to apply to worker safety within our own countries. Because work and environmental conditions vary from country to country, it is simply inappropriate to apply U.S. standards. Indeed, what is safe in the United States could be unsafe in another country. Second, the U.S. government must regulate product quality by specifically examining product quality as our apples arrive in the United States. The issue here is not the techniques of growing and harvesting, but rather whether the product is safe for the consumer. The U.S. government should test for that directly. If they did this, they would find that our apples are perfectly safe, even though we do not use the same production techniques used in the United States. The emphasis of the U.S. government on production techniques is misplaced—it is an effort to protect its domestic apple growers by raising our costs of production or forcing us to cease exporting to the United States.

8. With a price elasticity of demand for imports of 1, the 50 percent tariff rate has resulted in a 50 percent reduction in imports. The net national loss of the tariff as a percentage of the country's GDP equals (½)·0.50·0.50·0.20, or 2.5 percent. The increase in producer surplus in the protected sectors, as percentage of GDP, is approximately the 50 percent increase in domestic price times the 15 percent share of these sectors in GDP, or 7.5 percent. Thus, the net national loss from the tariff is about 33 percent of the gain to protected producers. For every dollar that domestic producers gain, the rest of the society loses $1.33.

10. Free trade will bring the largest well-being for the entire world. The United States already has few barriers against imports, and we believe that open competition has made the U.S. economy strong. But other countries often have protectionist policies. This hurts the U.S. economy, because we lose export opportunities that would allow us to take maximum benefits from our comparative advantages. Protectionist policies in foreign countries

usually also impose net national costs for those countries, and they certainly harm consumers in those countries. The protectionist policies exist to benefit certain producer groups in those countries, at the expense of others in the countries.

Section 301 is a tool that the U.S. government can use to reduce foreign protectionism and reduce or eliminate unfair foreign trade practices. Yes, it does involve threats by the U.S. government to raise its own import barriers if the foreign government does not lower its barriers, but this is a useful risk to take. The United States is large enough to influence foreign countries' governments, and the power here is being used for the good of the world. It is successful much of the time. When it is successful, the world moves toward freer trade, bringing benefits to the United States, to the foreign countries through net gains from freer trade, and to the world as a whole.

Chapter 9

Arguments for and against Protection

Overview

This chapter has two purposes: To present a framework and a rule for evaluating arguments offered in favor of limiting imports, and to apply the framework and rule to several prominent arguments for protection. The framework allows us to look at situations in which the free market may not result in economic efficiency, because of incentive distortions that result in market failures. In the "first-best" world with no distortions, private marginal benefits (MB) to consumers who make buying decisions equal social marginal benefits (SMB), because there are no consumption externalities or spillovers, private marginal costs (MC) recognized by sellers equal social marginal costs (SMC), because there are no production externalities or spillovers, and all of these are equal to market price, because the market is perfectly competitive and there are no distorting taxes. When external cost, external benefits, a distorting tax, monopoly power, or monopsony power exists, the market will usually not yield the first-best outcome, because social marginal benefit will not equal social marginal cost. In situations in which the free-market outcome is second-best, there is a potential role for government policy to contribute to economic efficiency. We mention the approach of creating new property rights, but we focus in this chapter on the tax-or-subsidy approach to eliminate distortions in private incentives.

Fortunately, there is a useful rule that works well in most cases. If the problem is an incentive distortion, the specificity rule indicates that government policy should intervene at the source of the problem, to act as directly as possible on the source of the distortion. (Toward the end of the chapter, we offer a second version of the specificity rule. If the government has a noneconomic objective, the government policy to achieve this noneconomic objective with the least economic cost is usually the policy that acts directly to achieve it.)

The specificity rule is powerful in its applications. If the problem is that a distortion results in too little domestic production, what is the best government policy to address the distortion? A tariff can be used to increase domestic production, so it may be better than doing nothing, but it is not the direct policy, because it acts on imports directly, not on domestic production. The best government policy is a subsidy to domestic production. Domestic production is increased, correcting the distortion. The production subsidy is better because it does not distort domestic consumption. A tariff would squeeze some consumers out of buying, resulting in the inefficiency of the consumption effect (triangle d). The tariff is indirect and not the best policy to address the production distortion. In fact, if we can be more specific about exactly what the source of the distortion is, we should employ a more specific policy. If the distortion arises from external benefits (e.g., training or acquiring better work habits) to working in the industry, then the best government policy acts directly, by subsidizing employment or training in the industry.

The infant industry argument leads to another application of the specificity rule, as well as raising a set of other interesting issues. The argument is that import competition prevents an initially uncompetitive domestic industry from starting production. But, if the industry is shielded from foreign competition, it can begin production, and over time it will be able to lower its production costs, so that it becomes competitive. At that time in the future the protection can be removed, and the industry will provide national benefits in the form of producer surplus. In this scenario, a tariff can be better than doing nothing, for national well-being over the long term. But the specificity rule indicates that the better government policy is one that acts directly on the source of distortion. If the issue is to foster initial domestic production, then a production subsidy is a better government policy. One may even wonder why this is needed. Why cannot the firms in the infant industry borrow to finance initial losses and then pay back the loans using future profits when the industry is grown up? If there are defects in the lending markets, then the government could extend loans. If the industry will create external benefits, such as training workers or new technologies, then the best government policy acts directly on the source of the external benefits (for instance, subsidies to training, or subsidies to research and development).

Another argument in favor of protection is assistance to industries that are declining because of rising import competition. Moving resources out of an industry is costly. People who lose their jobs because of increased imports often have a difficult time finding new jobs and often suffer substantial declines in earnings. The marginal social side benefit of continuing domestic production in this industry is avoiding these costs of moving resources to other uses. Again, a tariff can be used to maintain domestic production, and it may be better than doing nothing (so that the industry shrinks). But again the specificity says to attack the externality directly. A subsidy to domestic production will be better than a tariff, and other policies like subsidizing retraining of workers can be even better (more direct). The U.S. government does offer adjustment assistance to some workers who lose their jobs because of rising imports. Unfortunately, the retraining offered through this program is generally not that effective.

A different argument in favor of protection is that the government gains revenue. For a poor country with a weak tax system, the lack of government revenue can lead to inadequate supply of public goods (disease control, schooling, infrastructure). Tariffs and taxes on exports may be some of the few taxes that the government can collect effectively—they are a direct response to the source of the distortion. The benefits from better public goods can be much larger that the deadweight losses from the trade taxes. While this is potentially a valid argument for taxing trade, there is no guarantee that the government will use the revenues to fund socially useful investments. And as the country develops, it should shift toward broader-based taxes that are less distorting.

The chapter concludes with a look at several arguments in favor of protection that involve national pursuit of "noneconomic objectives." National pride gained by production of a product calls for a production subsidy as the least-cost way to achieve the objective. National pride in self-sufficiency calls for a tariff or other import limit, because in this case the objective is specifically to reduce or eliminate imports. Income redistribution is best achieved through income taxes and transfers. Providing for the national defense is usually least costly using a subsidy to domestic production capacity, leaving depletable resources in the ground, or building stockpiles. In the latter two cases imports can be part of the solution, if they are the least costly to acquire items during peacetime for consumption or to build up the stockpiles.

Tips

This chapter builds on the analysis of Chapters 7 and 8, but the flavor of the analysis is different. Students who like conceptual depth but dislike graphs will find relief here. The spotlight is now on the ideas, with the geometry more in the shadows. Logic still rules, but it is now more verbal and less mechanical.

Role playing can be used to bring the issues raised in the chapter to life. For instance, the class can be divided in half, with each half taking the opposite side in a debate about an actual trade problem. One possible topic: To protect U.S. jobs and raise the low U.S. wages in the clothing manufacturing sector, the U.S. government should tighten quotas or raise tariffs on imported clothing drastically. Another possible topic: The Japanese government should sell its scarce rights to land international flights at its airports to the highest bidders, even if this means that some Japanese airlines go out of business. Yet another: Brazil should limit its imports of personal computers, in order to foster the development of its own personal computer industry. Current events can offer other topics.

Suggested answers to questions and problems
(in the textbook)

2. The specificity rule is a guide to government policy that tries to enhance economic efficiency by addressing incentive distortions or market failures. It states that it is more efficient to use a policy that is closest to the source of a distortion separating private and social benefit or cost. It is also useful as a guide to government policy that tries to achieve a noneconomic objective with the least economic cost. For a noneconomic objective, it is least costly to use a policy that acts directly to achieve the objective.

4. The infant industry argument states that a country can benefit by shielding an industry (the infant) that is currently uncompetitive against foreign rivals, if that industry can lower its costs over time and become competitive in the future. It is potentially a valid argument for the government to do something to assist the infant industry, because the future benefits can be larger than the current costs of doing so. But, it has a number of weaknesses. First, even if some form of government assistance is appropriate, the specificity rule indicates that the best form of assistance is not a tariff or other barrier to imports. Rather, a subsidy to initial production or to whatever is the source of cost reductions over time is usually the best policy. Second, if the industry is so promising, it is often the case that no government assistance to the initial firms is needed. Instead, these firms should borrow from private lenders to cover their initial losses and repay these loans from future profits. Third, the argument is subject to abuse, because it is speculative. Will the industry really grow up—lower its costs to become competitive over time?

6.   The national defense argument states that the government must limit imports during peacetime to be assured that the country can meet its needs for defense goods during times of war. While the need to provide for the national defense is clear, the specificity rule says to think clearly about what the actual problems are, and then use policies that act directly on them. If the need is for production capabilities for a product, then the government should subsidize production capacity. If the need is for materials that can be stockpiled, then the government should build these. If the need is for access to depletable mineral resources, then the government should forego domestic production during peacetime, but have production capability ready if needed. Barriers to imports would achieve some of these objectives, but at a higher economic cost. In fact, imports during peacetime may be part of the solution, for building stockpiles or acquiring depletable resources so that domestic supplies are not used up.

8. a.   1. The tariff would raise the domestic price from the world price P_0 to the tariff-inclusive price P_1. Domestic production increases from S_0 to S_1, and domestic consumption falls from D_0 to D_1.

        2. By increasing domestic production from S_0 to S_1, the country gains social side benefits (worker training and skills) equal to area g.

        3. The tariff causes the usual production and consumption inefficiencies equal to areas b and d. The net gain or loss to the country is the difference between area g and areas (b + d).

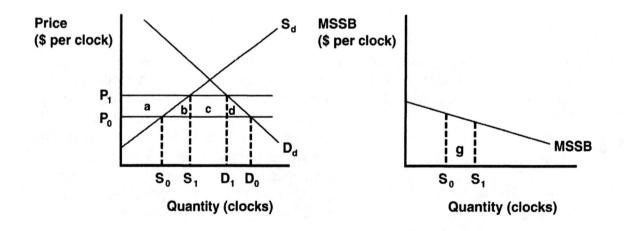

4. With a production subsidy instead of a tariff, the market price remains at P_0. Domestic consumption remains at D_0. Producers receive revenue per unit produced equal to P_1, which includes both the market price and the government subsidy per unit produced. They increase domestic production from S_0 to S_1. By increasing domestic production from S_0 to S_1, the country gains social side benefits (worker training and skills) equal to area g. The production subsidy causes a production inefficiency equal to area b, but it does not distort domestic consumption. The net national gain or loss to the country is the difference between area g and area b. As we expect from the specificity rule, the production subsidy is the better policy—it creates a larger net economic gain (or smaller economic loss) for the country, because it acts more directly on the source of the incentive distortion.

5. The tariff creates revenue for the government equal to area c. The production subsidy creates a cost to the government equal to area (a + b). The deficit-conscious finance minister, looking only at the government budget, would favor the tariff.

    b.   The specificity rule indicates that the best policy is to subsidize or support worker training directly.

10.   The interests of the sock exporting countries are probably to export a large quantity of socks and to receive a high price for the socks that are exported. Presume that the sock importing countries are going to use one of these policies to achieve a specific target quantity of domestic sock production. Consider first the effect on quantity of sock imports/exports. To achieve the target domestic production in the sock importing countries, the tariff and the VER would reduce sock imports by the same amount. But a production subsidy in the importing countries could achieve the same production objective with a smaller reduction in sock imports, because domestic consumers continue to be able to buy socks at the world price and do not cut back on their purchases. The sock exporting countries would tend to favor the production subsidy, because it results in a smaller decrease in the quantity that they export. Consider next the effect on the price received by the sock exporters. Both the tariff and the production subsidy reduce sock import demand, so that they would tend to put downward pressure on sock export prices. (The downward pressure is larger for the tariff, because the reduction in sock imports is larger.) The VER could be used by the exporting countries to form a kind of sock exporting cartel and raise export prices. The sock exporting countries would tend to favor the VER, because it will "force" them to raise sock export prices. Overall, the sock exporting countries would rate the tariff as the least desirable. Their rating of the production subsidy and the VER would depend on their priority between a smaller reduction in quantity exported (favors the production subsidy) or a higher price for sock exports (favors the VER).

Chapter 10

Pushing Exports

Overview

Chapters 7 through 9 focused on government policies toward imports, with little attention to government policies and business practices in the exporting countries. This chapter shifts to looking at various practices and policies that can increase exports, as well as the effects of these export-promoting activities on importing countries. The chapter has four major purposes:

1. Examine dumping—what it is, why it occurs, how it affects importing countries, and what government policies are used in importing countries.
2. Examine export subsidies, looking at the same set of issues.
3. Examine actual experience in six industries in which government policies may have helped new exporters.
4. Look at recent evidence on whether the Japanese government used industrial targeting to promote Japan's export industries of the future.

Dumping is selling exports at a price that is "too low." There are two standards sanctioned by WTO rules: selling exports at a price that is lower than the price in the home market (or in third country markets), or selling exports at a price that is lower than the full average cost of production (including a profit margin). The legal standard is one or the other, not both.

There are at least four different reasons that a exporter would dump (based on one or the other of the two definitions). Predatory dumping is intended to drive out rivals. Cyclical dumping occurs during an industry downturn in demand, with sales below average cost. Seasonal dumping unloads excess inventories, especially on products that are perishable or going out of fashion. Persistent dumping is international price discrimination, with the exporting firm facing a less elastic demand curve in the home market, and having some way to limit or prevent reimport back into its home market.

What should the importing country think of dumping? The first reaction should be to welcome it—why argue if someone is willing to sell you something at a low price? This seems to be the best reaction to both seasonal and persistent dumping. The importing country could have additional concerns about cyclical dumping. If used aggressively, it can export unemployment. Predatory dumping is potentially the most troubling to the importing country. If the exporter succeeds, it will raise prices in the future, and the importing country can be harmed. But predatory dumping probably rare.

Actual importing-country government policies toward dumping generally do not make these economically sensible distinctions. The policy usually investigates alleged dumping by looking at whether the export price is too low, by either standard, and looking at whether there is injury to domestic industry. If both are found, then the importing country imposes antidumping duties equal to the difference between the low export price and the "normal price" or "fair market value." The policy does not look at the overall effect of alleged dumping on the national well-being of the importing country, because it does not examine the effects on domestic consumers, and it does not attempt to determine the reason for the dumping. It appears that the process is biased in favor of finding dumping and imposing antidumping duties. And even the threat of a dumping suit can induce foreign exporters to raise their prices. Antidumping policy has become a way for import-competing producers to gain new protection against imports.

Governments in exporting countries sometimes use export subsidies to increase their exports. These export subsidies create inefficiency by distorting domestic production, and they discriminate against consumers in the exporting countries. WTO rules generally prohibit export subsidies and permit importing countries to impose countervailing duties in response. We examine the peculiar economics of all of this, using the case in which the export subsidy lowers the price of exports, and the market is otherwise competitive. Because of the lower import price, the importing country gains well-being in the shift from free trade with no subsidy to free trade with the foreign export subsidy (and no countervailing duty). If the importing country then imposes a countervailing duty, the importing country still gains, in comparison with free trade with no subsidy and duty, but it does not gain as much as it would if it did not impose the duty.

The economics of an export subsidy are rather different if the market is not perfectly competitive—a major insight of strategic trade policy. The text shows the example of competition between Boeing and Airbus for the world market for a new type of airplane. With no government support, it is possible that neither firm will enter the new market, because both will lose if both enter. But if one government offers a suitable subsidy, its firm will enter. If the other government does not offer support, then the other firm will not enter, and the first firm will earn high profits, bringing a benefit to its country and possibly to the entire world. But, if the other government also offers a subsidy, both firms produce. The world's consumers gain, but each of the producing countries can end up with lower well-being because of its firm's loss net of the government subsidy (the subsidy is a transfer within the country).

The chapter then turns to looking at how big a role government support has actually played in aiding the rise of new exporters in six industries. The analysis is simply looking at whether government assistance played an important role. It is not a full analysis of whether the government assistance increased net national well-being. In three of these sectors—steel, automobiles, and apparel—government played a small role. In television and semiconductors, Japanese government support played some role, but it probably was not large, and the Japanese industries recently have suffered some reversals. In aircraft, government support was large, and it has had the effect of establishing the U.S. industry (Boeing) as the leader and the European industry (Airbus) as the effective challenger.

The chapter concludes with a look at recent evidence on Japanese government assistance to industry. The evidence shows that the Japanese government has not had a coherent industrial targeting policy that has favored high-growth industries that can succeed as exporters. Rather, relatively larger amounts of various types of government assistance have tended to go to slower growing industries in Japan.

Tips

There is much here to interest the student who gravitates toward policy debate or business relevance. There are often current cases of alleged dumping (e.g., steel in the United States) that can be incorporated into class discussion. This is also a natural place to incorporate additional reading on East Asia's industrial development.

The material, especially that on dumping, can lead to lively class discussion. For instance, the instructor can present the legal definitions of dumping, and then ask students why an exporting firm would engage in dumping. The follow-up question can be to ask what the importing country should think of dumping.

In a course that cannot cover all of the material in this chapter, it does have separable parts. For instance, the instructor can emphasize economic analysis by assigning the sections on dumping and antidumping policies, export subsidies and countervailing duties, strategic export subsidies, and perhaps also Japan's industrial targeting.

Suggested answers to questions and problems
(in the textbook)

2. The objectives of the revision should be make antidumping policy contribute to U. S. national well-being. The policy should be targeted toward predatory dumping and aggressive cyclical dumping. It should take into account domestic consumer interests as well as domestic producer interests. It generally should not impose antidumping duties on persistent dumping that involves international price discrimination in favor of U.S. buyers. The specific provisions could include the following. First, the definition of dumping should be changed. Dumping should be defined as pricing an export below the average variable cost (or marginal cost) of production. This change will permit the definition of dumping to be focused on overly aggressive pricing that is often characteristic of predatory dumping or aggressive cyclical dumping. Second, the test for injury should include consideration of benefits to domestic consumers from low-priced imports, in addition to harm to domestic producers. The injury test should be a test of effect on net national well-being. A radical alternative is to abolish the antidumping law, and instead focus on prosecuting any predatory dumping using U.S. antitrust laws that prohibit monopolization.

4. A countervailing duty is a tariff imposed to offset the amount by which a foreign government subsidizes its exports to the country imposing the duty.

6. a. With free trade, price is P_0 and the quantity exported and imported is M_0. The export subsidy "artificially" shifts the export supply curve down to S_X'. (The original S_X curve still shows the resource cost of exports, but the foreign exporters are willing to sell at the lower market prices shown by S_X' because the foreign government also pays them the

export subsidy.) The international market price falls to P_1 and the quantity traded increases to M_1.

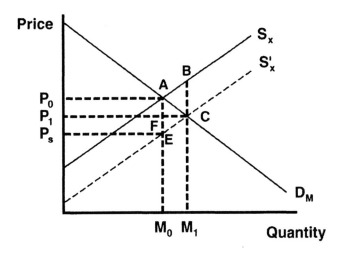

b.   The countervailing duty returns the market to P_0 and M_0. This is good for the world, because the marginal resource cost of the last unit exported (shown by the height of S_x at M_0) just equals the marginal benefit of that unit to the buyer (shown by the height of D_M at M_0). We return to the economic efficiency of the free-trade outcome. The export subsidy alone caused a global economic inefficiency equal to triangle ABC, the inefficiency of too much exporting. In comparison with just the export subsidy, the countervailing duty can increase the well-being of the importing country, in the same way that a tariff can increase the well-being of a large country. By imposing the countervailing duty, the importing country loses triangle ACF and gains rectangle P_1FEP_S. The importing country gains if the rectangle is larger than the triangle.

8.   No, according to careful recent research. Instead the Japanese government tends to provide relatively greater assistance to the slower-growing industries in the economy.

10.   One way is to say that most actual and potential export industries are highly competitive. In this case, export subsidies distort resource allocation within the economy, leading to overproduction of the exportable goods. The export subsidies bring a national net loss, with the case of Korean steel as an example. Another example is Europe's development of the Concorde, an airplane that almost no airlines bought, because it was uneconomic

even with the subsidies. The counter to the infant industry argument is that in most cases the infant fails to grow up, so the country then faces the choice of whether or not to provide ongoing assistance to a high-cost, uncompetitive industry.

Chapter 11

Trade Blocs and Trade Blocks

Overview

This chapter examines two types of trade barriers that are intended to discriminate between foreign countries. A trade bloc has lower or no barriers for trade between its members, while they maintain higher barriers for trade with outside countries. A trade embargo or trade block places extra barriers against trade with a specific foreign country, usually because of a broader policy disagreement.

There are four major types of trade or economic blocs: free-trade area, customs union, common market, and economic union. We usually analyze trade blocs by comparing them to countries maintaining barriers against all other countries. WTO rules generally call for equal trade barriers against all other countries (at least those that are also members of the WTO)—the most-favored-nation principle. But the WTO rules also have a few exceptions, including an exception for a trade bloc that achieves substantially free trade among its members.

A trade bloc can have several effects on the well-being of its member countries and the world overall. If forming or joining the trade bloc results in lower prices in the importing member country, the country and the world gain as additional trade is created. If forming or joining the trade bloc results in shifting the source of imports into the country from low-priced suppliers from countries outside the trade bloc to higher-priced partner suppliers, the country and the world lose as trade is diverted from low-cost to higher-cost producers. The net effect depends on whether the gains from trade creation are larger than the losses from trade diversion. There are also possible dynamic gains from forming or joining a trade bloc, including gains if economies of scale are achieved within the larger free-trade area and gains if extra competition within the area leads to better productivity, lower costs, or greater innovation.

For the European Union, most estimates are that the EU gains from its internal free trade in manufactures, because trade creation has been larger than trade diversion, and because there are probably also dynamic gains, although these are harder to measure. Additional gains came as the move to a truly common market in 1992 removed nontariff barriers and freed resource movements. However, the EU also incurs substantial losses from its highly protectionist common agricultural policy.

The North American Free Trade Area (NAFTA) began in 1994, subsuming the previous Canada-U.S. Free Trade Area. NAFTA eliminates tariffs, reduces some nontariff barriers, and liberalizes trade in services and cross-border business investments. The formation of NAFTA was controversial. In Mexico there were fears of jobs lost to more productive U.S. and Canadian firms, as well as the loss of political sovereignty as NAFTA committed Mexico to change a number of its government policies. In the United States there were fears of job losses to low-wage Mexico, as well as complaints about linking with a country that has a corrupt political system and poor environmental protection. Proponents in both Mexico and the United States hoped that NAFTA would commit the Mexican government to maintain and extend its market-oriented reforms. Estimates indicate that Mexico may gain substantially from the formation of NAFTA, with relatively smaller gains for the United States. Estimates suggest that Canada gained from the formation of the Canada-U.S. Free Trade Area, partly from trade creation and probably partly by achieving scale economies as access to the large U.S. market became assured. Canada had small additional gains from NAFTA. NAFTA is also likely to alter the distribution of income within each country. For instance, less-skilled labor-intensive industries in the United States are likely to face additional pressure from Mexican competition.

For decades efforts to form functioning trade blocs among developing countries failed. Success is now more likely, as many developing countries have shifted toward outward-oriented and market-oriented government policies. MERCOSUR (the Southern Common Market) began in 1991 and has been largely successful in freeing internal trade and establishing common external tariffs. Yet, there are some fears that it has also led to substantial trade diversion.

A trade embargo is economic warfare. It hurts both the target country and the country imposing the trade block, and it creates opportunities for other countries that are not taking part in the embargo. An embargo can fail to force the target country to change its policy for at least two reasons. First, the target country's national decision makers may decide that they can and must endure their losses, even if these losses are large—political failure of an embargo. Second, the embargo may simply fail to inflict much loss on the target country—economic failure of an embargo. An embargo that prohibits exports to the target country is more likely to succeed economically when the target country has an inelastic demand for imports and countries outside the embargo have low elasticities of export supply. This is more likely when a group of large countries impose an embargo on a small country, and when the embargo is sudden and extreme.

Tips

The unifying theme is trade discrimination, and the material is not too difficult. The diagrams represent fairly straightforward extensions from those in previous chapters.

In class presentation of trade blocs, it may be useful to present a case of pure trade creation (in which the partner country is the low-priced world supplier), a case of pure trade diversion (in which the partner's export price is just slightly less than the tariff-inclusive outsider price), and then the general case in which there is both trade creation and trade diversion.

There are two distinct parts to the chapter, and they are separable. For instance, an instructor can assign and cover only the material on trade blocs if there is a need to slim down the total course content.

Suggested answers to questions and problems

(in the textbook)

2.   The most favored nation principle states that any trade policy concession given by a country to any foreign country must be given to all other foreign countries having MFN status. WTO rules state that all WTO members are entitled to MFN status, but there are some exceptions.

4.   In a free trade area the member countries permit free trade among themselves but each maintains its own set of tariffs and nontariff barriers to imports from outside countries. Rules of origin are necessary to prevent outside countries from sending their exports into a low-barrier member country and then shipping these products on to a high-barrier member country, to circumvent the high barriers in this second member country. Rules of origin can be protectionist because they act like area-wide local content requirements. If a high local content is required, then it can force firms to use materials and components produced within the free trade area (rather than importing these items from outside the area).

6.   Mexico is likely to gain from NAFTA, as trade creation is likely to be larger than trade diversion, and Mexican firms also gain better access to selling to the large U.S. market. In Mexico, the gains will be largest for those sectors tied to exports and for those resources (including less-skilled labor) that are relatively abundant in Mexico. The United States and Canada are also likely to gain, with gains to those export sectors that can increase their sales to Mexico and to resources that are relatively abundant in these countries, including skilled labor. Outside countries are likely to be hurt by trade diversion, but estimates are that this effect is small.

8.   Trade embargoes are usually imposed by large countries that are important in the trade of the target country. An embargo has a better chance to succeed if it is imposed suddenly rather than gradually, because a sudden interruption of economic flows damages the target country by a large amount for some time before it can develop alternatives (in economic terms, for a good that the target imports, its import demand is inelastic in the short run, and the elasticity of alternative export supplies may be inelastic in the short run as well).

10.

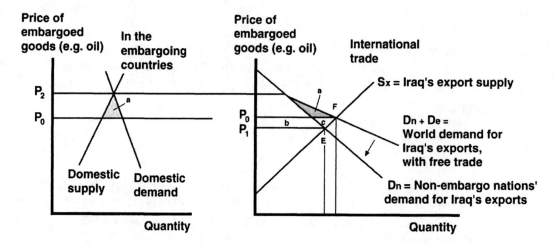

There are three relevant types of countries—the embargoing countries that otherwise would import, the non-embargo importing countries, and the target country (say, Iraq). Before the embargo (free trade), the world price is P_0. When the embargo is imposed, the price in the embargoing countries rises to P_2, and the price that Iraq gets for its exports to the non-embargo countries falls to P_1. The cost of the embargo to the embargoing countries is area a. The loss to Iraq from exporting less at a lower price is area (b + c). The embargo is more powerful if area (b + c) is larger, and this is larger if Iraq's export supply is less elastic, the non-embargo countries' import demand is less elastic, or the embargoing countries' import demand is more elastic. This last condition probably also makes it easier for embargoing countries to do without Iraq's products during the embargo, because area a is probably smaller.

Chapter 12

Trade and the Environment

Overview

We begin the chapter with two provocative questions. First, is free trade anti-environment? We argue that it is not. There is no reason to think that trade generally promotes production or consumption of products that cause large harm to the environment. Surprisingly, the incentive to relocate production into "pollution havens" is usually small. Trade tends to raise world incomes. While some environmental problems become worse as income rises, others become less severe, in part because protecting the environment is a luxury good. Second, is the World Trade Organization anti-environment? WTO rules recognize environmental-protection exceptions to its general thrust toward free trade, but the WTO is also worried that restrictions that claim to be necessary to protect the environment are pretexts for common protectionism. Countries can impose product standards to protect the environment, but they must apply to all consumption, not just imports, and they must be based on scientific evidence. The WTO generally has been unwilling to permit countries to limit imports because they are produced in foreign countries using methods that the importing country considers to be damaging to the environment.

Adverse environmental effects like pollution are negative externalities, distortions that lead to failures of the market to be fully efficient. The specificity rule introduced in Chapter 9 is a handy guide to government policy to address negative environmental externalities. In fact, there are two types of government policy that can directly attack the distortion—imposing taxes and subsidies, or changing property rights. As in Chapter 9, we usually use the tax-and-subsidy approach.

The specificity rule says to use the direct approach; for instance, tax pollution directly. If this is not possible, then the specificity rule says to select the tax or subsidy that is as close as possible to the act creating the pollution. An additional complication is that the source of the pollution can be our own country's activity, another country's activity, or the entire world's activity. If our country cannot achieve an international agreement, we may be left to take our own policy action, even though the source of much of the problem is foreign activity. In this case trade barriers could be a second-best policy that can enhance well-being. Figure 12.2 is a useful summary of the main conclusions that can drawn for the various possible cases.

In our formal analysis we begin with the case in which pollution caused by an activity within the country has effects only on this country. We use tools similar to those that we developed in Chapter 9. If the country simply allows the pollution to occur, with no government policy to limit the negative externality, we show that free trade can make the country worse off, and that the country can export the wrong products. This occurs because of the marginal social side costs, in our example resulting from pollution that accompanies domestic production of the export good. A government policy that taxes pollution or production that causes pollution (or that establishes suitable property rights) can reverse these effects, assuring that the country exports and imports the appropriate products and gains from free international trade.

Domestic producers subject to the pollution-related tax may complain that other countries, especially the countries that become the suppliers of the country's imports, are not imposing a comparable pollution-related tax on their firms. They may complain that the foreign firms are engaged in "eco-dumping." From the perspective of the importing country, lax foreign controls should not matter to its well-being, as long as the foreign pollution does not affect it.

The analysis of transborder pollution raises new issues. We use the example of production activity in one country that pollutes a river flowing into a neighboring country. The best solution would balance the gains to the polluting country from dumping waste into the river with the costs of pollution to the receiving country. Generally, this best solution is less pollution than the amount that occurs with no government policy, but more than zero pollution. However, the government in the polluting country may resist imposing a pollution tax (or some other way to limit pollution by its firms), because it bears the national costs while the other country gets the national benefits. If international negotiations fail, what should the receiving country do? It cannot tax the foreign pollution or even the foreign production that causes pollution. If the receiving country imports the product from the polluting country, it could try to reduce the foreign production and pollution by restricting its imports. The country will gain if its benefits from lower foreign pollution exceed the usual deadweight losses of protection. (If instead the receiving country is an exporter of this product to the polluting country, it could subsidize its exports.) However, the WTO generally interprets its environmental exceptions narrowly, so it is not clear that the WTO would uphold the import restriction (or export subsidy), if the polluting country complained to the WTO.

The difficulty of addressing transborder pollution is also shown through a discussion of the slow progress that NAFTA has made in attempting to ameliorate environmental problems along the Mexico-U.S. border. In addition, the box on "Dolphins, Turtles, and the WTO" discusses two cases in which the WTO ruled against U.S. import restrictions intended to force foreign fishing fleets to adopt methods that reduce killing of dolphins and sea turtles.

Some environmental problems are global—the whole world's economic activity imposes an external cost on the whole world. Each country might be willing to make some effort to reduce its own pollution, because it recognizes that its own activities have some adverse effect on itself. But each country on its own would not decrease enough, because it would not recognize the costs that its pollution imposes on other countries. Yet the world, and most countries, would be better off if the countries cooperated to reduce the pollution more. Such global agreements are difficult to achieve, because of disagreements about the how serious the problem is, the incentive to free-ride, and the difficulty of enforcement.

The chapter concludes with four examples of global environmental problems. The Convention on International Trade in Endangered Species of Wild Fauna and Flora attempts to prevent extinction of species by restricting or banning commercial trade in threatened species. It has been reasonably effective. But it may need to shift toward encouraging sustainable use of many threatened species, through economic management of the species for commercial uses.

Overfishing is an example of the tragedy of the commons. It does not threaten extinction for most species, but rather it results in fish catches that are smaller than they could be. We pay a global cost for our inability to conclude effective international agreements to prevent overfishing.

Release of chlorofluorocarbons (CFCs) has resulted in ozone depletion. The Montreal Protocol, signed in 1987, is an example of an effective international agreement. It began with restrictions on trade in CFCs and has spread to reduction of production of CFCs. It has been successful in reducing the buildup of CFCs in the atmosphere and replacing CFCs with less harmful alternatives.

The buildup of carbon dioxide and other greenhouse gasses in the atmosphere, and the likelihood that this is causing global warning, is perhaps the largest global environmental challenge. We cannot use science to predict exactly how much global warming will occur. The scientific uncertainty probably argues for taking moderate steps as "insurance" while awaiting better information. However, three palatable policy options—removing energy subsidies, planting new forests, and waiting for scarcity to raise the prices of fossil fuels—would have effects that are too small to help much. Furthermore, the specific problem is clearly not international trade in fossil fuels or other sources of greenhouse gases. The problem is the worldwide activity, especially burning fossil fuels, that releases greenhouse gases. A policy response consistent with the specificity rule is to tax consumption (or production) of fossil fuels on a nearly global scale. But an international agreement to impose such a tax appears to be impossible to achieve. Actual global negotiations so far have been disappointing. Developing countries have refused to make any commitments. Industrialized countries have made commitments to reduce their greenhouse gas emissions. However, it is unlikely that the U.S. Congress will enact laws to meet the U.S. commitments, so the agreements are unlikely to accomplish much.

Tips

The material of this chapter lends itself to additional examples. The instructor can introduce extra material in lecture, in class handouts, or in additional readings. Some examples include the threat to the marine population of the Galapagos, acid rain in Eastern Europe, water quality and air quality along the Rio Grande, or the U.S. diversion of water in the Colorado River before it gets to Mexico. You may also find useful global data in the *World Resources* periodical of the World Resources Institute, cited in Appendix A of the textbook.

As interesting examples are included in the discussion, we recommend keeping economic principles in full view. It is useful to remind students that:
- incentive distortions and imperfect property rights are crucial causes of environmental problems, whether these problems are international or not;
- there are two basic policy approaches—the (Pigovian) tax-and-subsidy approach, and the (Coasian) property-rights approach;

- we keep discovering new uses for the specificity rule introduced in Chapter 9; and
- this rule almost never recommends trade policy as a first-best approach to environmental problems.

Suggested answers to questions and problems

(in the textbook)

2. Disagree. The distortion caused by pollution is the result of the difference between the private costs and the social costs of the activity that creates the pollution. Because the person choosing to take an action that creates pollution does not care about the social side costs of the pollution, he tends to create too much pollution. Free trade does not alter the fact the there will remain a gap between private cost and the social cost (inclusive of the cost of pollution).

4. The first thing to consider is whether the mine-related pollution in the lax countries has any adverse environmental effect on the strict country. If it does not, then the strict country has no national concern about lax policies in other countries. The strict country should get its own environmental policies right. If it can import ores cheaply from lax countries, then this increases its national gains from trade. If the mine-related pollution does have an adverse effect on the strict country, then the official should be concerned, not because the lax policies are unfair, but rather because of the external cost imposed on the country. The government in the strict country should negotiate with the lax country government for appropriate regulations. If these fail, the strict country government might benefit from imposing limits on imports of ores from the lax countries, because this would lower the production and pollution created in the lax countries.

6. a. The shaded loss area b is now $15 million. Free trade makes the country better off, because the usual gain from trade (area a, equal to $25 million) is larger than the loss from increased pollution ($15 million).

   b. If there is no way to reduce pollution per ream of paper produced, then the first-best outcome can be achieved if the government imposes a tax of $0.05 per ream produced domestically. This shifts the domestic supply curve up to (S_d + $0.05). The country should still export paper, but the amount that it should export is less. With the tax, the country will produce 2.15 billion reams domestically at the international price $1.10, so it will export 350 million reams.

8. a. The governments should determine the social side costs imposed by the pollution on both countries combined, and impose this as a tax per unit of pollution emitted by the cement producers. When the tax is imposed, the cement producers will adopt the lower-pollution technology, if its cost is less than the tax. The price of cement will increase as the tax and the new technology (if adopted) increase the costs recognized by the cement producers. Pollution will decline to its appropriate level (probably not zero) because the higher price reduces quantity demanded, so production declines, as well as because pollution is lower if the new technology is adopted.

b. If the Pugelovian government must fashion a solution on its own, it should consider restricting its imports of cement from Lindertania. This is not the first-best solution. It does not create any incentive to adopt the lower-pollution technology. But it can lower Lindertania's production, so pollution will be lower. This brings a net gain to Pugelovia if the gains from lower pollution are greater than the usual losses from restricting imports.

10. The success of the Montreal Convention in limiting CFCs was largely due to these facts: (a) the scientific evidence that CFCs were depleting the ozone was clear; (b) relatively few countries and companies accounted for most of the world's production of CFCs, limiting the number of negotiating parties; (c) these countries were located at high altitudes, where the danger of ozone depletion was greatest; (d) these countries were rich and therefore relatively willing to make economic sacrifices to protect the environment; and (e) reasonable substitutes for CFCs became available. The conditions surrounding the emission of carbon dioxide and other greenhouse gases are not as favorable. The science that links greenhouse gases to global warming is less certain. The burning of fossil fuels does concentrate somewhat in the richer countries, especially the United States, but all countries burn fuels and release greenhouse gases, and the emissions are growing fastest in some of the developing countries. There are no reasonable and acceptable substitutes that can be used on a large scale to replace the burning of fossil fuels for energy and heat. Because the conditions are less favorable, the negotiations over an agreement to limit the emission of greenhouse gases have been relatively unproductive.

Chapter 13

Trade Policies for Developing and Transition Countries

Overview

This chapter examines trade issues affecting developing countries. It begins by noting differences between high-income developed or industrialized countries and low- and medium-income developing countries, as well as differences among the developing countries. Some developing countries are growing quickly, while others are stagnating or declining. In addition, the developing countries of Central and Eastern Europe and the former Soviet Union are in the process of transition from communist central planning.

Developing countries are different from developed countries in at least three ways. First, their factor endowments are different. They have less nonhuman capital and fewer human skills. Some have raw materials, and many have a tropical climate. Second, their financial capital markets work less efficiently. Third, their labor markets work less efficiently. Given these differences, a developing country must decide what trade policy (and other government policies) to adopt. It can adopt free trade so that its exports are market-determined and based on the country's comparative advantage. It can adopt a policy that taxes exports, to try to raise world prices for its export goods or to raise government revenues that can used to develop other parts of its economy. It can tax and restrict imports to develop new domestic industries through import substitution. It can promote and subsidize new export products. Given the less efficient capital and labor markets, there may be a role for an active government trade policy.

Import-substituting industrialization (ISI) was the dominant policy in the 1950s and 1960s, and it is still important today. At its best, it is an application of the infant-industry argument, guided by the existence of a market for the goods produced by the new domestic producers, with tariff revenues that may be justified by the developing-government argument, and it can also improve the country's terms of trade by reducing demand for imports. However, because the terms of trade effects are usually small, it imposes substantial economic costs through deadweight losses—it often results in domestic industries that have high costs, domestic monopoly power, and low-quality products. Countries like Taiwan and South Korea that have shifted from a policy of ISI to a more outward-oriented policy that encourages development through exporting usually grow faster with the outward-oriented policy, and comparison of countries that had outward-oriented polices with those that practiced ISI shows that the former grew more quickly on average.

Some developing countries rely on primary products for most of their exports. Evidence indicates that these countries appear to have experienced a slow deterioration in their terms of trade over time. It appears that the adverse effects of Engel's Law and the development of synthetic substitutes has been more important than the limits of natural scarcity and slow growth of productivity in primary-goods production. The conclusions are tentative, because there are biases in the data—declining transport costs, faster unmeasured quality improvements for manufactured goods, and the difficulty of incorporating new manufactured products into the price comparisons.

One possible approach to the problem of declining primary product prices is to form international cartels to raise their prices. OPEC did this for oil in the 1970s. The analysis of a cartel as a group that has monopoly power because it controls a large part of the world's production indicates the limits to this power and why cartels usually erode over time. Demand becomes more elastic over time, new competing supplies from outside the cartel enter the market, increasing the noncartel supply elasticity and decreasing the cartel's market share, and cheating by cartel members often increases over time. Outside of oil, the prospects for even temporary success of primary product cartels seems poor, and there are currently no effective cartels.

Developing countries have turned increasingly toward emphasizing new exports of manufactured goods to industrialized countries as their trade policy to promote development. The success of this policy can be limited by protectionism in the industrialized countries, but reasonable success is still possible.

The transition from communist central planning to a market economy poses special challenges for the trade and other policies of the transition countries. Under central planning the countries strove for self-sufficiency and directed their trade to other centrally planned countries. A key question is speed—should the policy transition be fast or slow? The Central and Eastern European countries and the Baltic countries pursued rapid liberalizations. The other countries of the former Soviet Union were more gradual. A key challenge is redirecting exports toward Western Europe and other market economy countries. The Central and Eastern European countries and Estonia among the Baltics have been more successful in reorienting exports. Transition will be disruptive and national output will decline under any set of government policies. The evidence indicates that rapid liberalization, with its quick shift to freer trade, world market prices, and more intense competition, brings substantial gains in economic efficiency and a quicker return to positive growth rates of national output.

Tips

The chapter is designed so that the instructor can emphasize some policy issues more than others, if this is desired. The introduction and first section provide the setting. Most courses probably will include the theory and practice of ISI, and comparisons with outward-oriented policies. This is a topic on which much evidence has been gathered since the 1970s, with a relatively clear consensus against the earlier hopes for the ISI strategy. The Asian crisis beginning in 1997 has temporarily set back many of the leaders of the outward-oriented policies. With the exception of Indonesia, these economies seem to be returning to growth by mid-1999. Most courses also probably will want to cover the section on "Exports of Manufactures to Industrial Countries," because this follows from the discussion of outward-oriented policies.

By contrast, the middle sections on primary products and cartels may be omitted if it is necessary to conserve time for other topics. The final section on transition economies might also be omitted, but this section is likely to be of noticeable interest to many students, because the end of communist central planning is fairly recent and the problems of countries like Russia remain in the news.

The annual *Transition Report* issued by the European Bank for Reconstruction and Development is an excellent sources of updated information on new policy developments and recent economic performance in the transition countries.

The second section of Appendix D has a technical treatment of optimal export taxes and the optimal markup for an international cartel.

Suggested answers to questions and problems
(in the textbook)

2. The four arguments in favor of ISI are the infant-industry argument, the developing-government argument, the chance to improve the terms of trade for a large importing country, and economizing on market information. The conditions under which ISI is likely to be better than alternative strategies include the following. First, being a large country is probably important, not only for the terms of trade effect, but also because a large domestic market makes it possible for a number of domestic firms to compete for sales while still achieving scale economies. Second, conditions favoring the maturing of infant industries, such as a trainable labor force or spillovers from technology brought into domestic production, are probably important. Third, it is probably useful for the government to have poor ability to raise revenues using more broadly based taxes, so that tariff revenues are important to the government budget. Fourth, it is probably useful that poor information makes evaluation of opportunities for successful export products difficult. ISI should be accompanied by investment in training and education, investment in domestic infrastructure such as roads and other domestic transportation facilities, and a competent and honest civil service.

4. Two forces are likely to drive toward a deteriorating terms of trade—a decrease in the prices of the primary product exports relative to the prices of the manufactured good imports. First, the global demand for primary products is likely to rise more slowly than the global demand for manufactured goods will rise, as global incomes rise, because primary products have lower income elasticities of demand (Engel's Law). Second, new synthetic substitutes are likely to be developed for some of the primary products, lowering global demand for the primary products. Two forces are likely to drive toward an improved terms of trade. First, natural limits could restrain global supply of some primary products. Second, slow growth in primary-product productivity is likely to limit cost decreases, so primary product prices do not fall as much as (or will rise more than) the cost and prices of manufactures that experience more rapid productivity growth. In addition, more rapid quality improvements in manufactured products effectively increase the country's terms of trade.

6.   First, taxing exports of primary products could improve the country's international terms of trade, if the country is large enough to affect international prices (the optimal export tax, the counterpart of the optimal import tariff presented in Chapter 7, and the national equivalent of the international cartel analyzed in this chapter). If there are net national gains, they are likely to be largest in the first years after the export tax is imposed, before the monopoly power of the country is eroded (in ways shown in the discussion of an international cartel). Second, taxing exports of primary products will induce resource reallocations to other production sectors, including manufactured goods that can replace imports and perhaps develop into new export industries. Third, the revenues from the export tax can be used to pay for national public goods like education and infrastructure. Or, these revenues can be used to subsidize infant industries that can develop into mature, internationally competitive industries in the future. Drawbacks loom large in practice. First, the country may lack monopoly power, in which case the export tax just distorts domestic resource allocation and creates deadweight losses. Second, the government often lacks information about which new industries to encourage. Third, the additional revenues are often siphoned off to the private wealth of government officials.

8.   The prediction is that the shift to an outward oriented policy will result in an increase in Argentina's growth rate, so that it is among the higher growth rates for developing countries. The data shown in Figure 13.1 is consistent with the prediction. Argentina's rate of growth of per capita GDP was 3.2 percent, among the higher growth rates shown for developing countries.

10. a.   Unilaterally taxing grain exports has the advantage of being collectible by a small customs staff at the nation's major border crossings, as in the developing-government argument. The export-tax revenues could be invested in public goods such as health, education, and infrastructure, or they could be used to subsidize other promising sectors of the economy. Ukraine probably cannot force up the world price of grain, because it is not large enough, given severe competition from other grain exporters.

   b.   An international grain cartel is politically unlikely and would break down almost immediately, given competition from suppliers that would stay outside the cartel and cheating by members of the cartel.

   c.   This classic infant-industry argument has possibilities, but all of Chapter 9's doubts about its wisdom are reinforced by this chapter's recitation of the evidence about how poorly ISI has worked in practice.

Chapter 14

The Political Economy of Trade and Agriculture

Overview

This chapter examines two issues: the political process that results in government policies toward trade and the rather unusual trade and other government policies toward agricultural products.

We believe that the political economy of trade policy can be examined by looking at five major elements:
- how much the winners gain from protection and how many benefit.
- how much the losers are harmed by protection and how many lose.
- what reasons individual people and companies have for taking positions for or against protection.
- what types of political activities people and companies can use and their costs.
- what the political institutions and processes are.

Tariffs and other trade barriers are unlikely under at least two combinations of these elements:
- when decisions are made by direct voting and people vote based on whether they are winners or losers from protection, or
- when individuals are willing to devote all of their gains from winning (for or against protection) to lobbying or contributions and elected representatives (or other government officials) decide on the basis of the amount of lobbying or contributions they receive.

Tariffs and other trade barriers are more likely to be adopted when the group that will gain from protection is better organized in its lobbying and contributions. In fact, we often expect that the group with the smaller number of individuals can be more effective, because the larger gain per individual is likely to result in more activity by the smaller group, and because the smaller group is more likely to find ways to overcome the free-rider problem. The small number of import-competing producers are motivated to participate and overcome the free-rider problem, so they become a well-organized group with substantial resources to use politically to seek protection. The outcome is that the well-organized protectionist lobby sways a majority of politicians to enact tariffs or other import barriers.

In addition to explaining the general political process that leads to protection, this model of political activity can explain several specific features of trade policy. Tariff escalation occurs because the buyers of materials and component are firms that can organize to oppose tariffs on these intermediate goods. Offers to reduce tariffs in a multilateral trade negotiation are called concessions because producer groups are politically powerful. In addition, sudden damage creates sympathy, so that even those who are hurt by protection sometimes say that they favor protection to assist those hurt by rising imports. In fact, given this discussion, the surprising thing is not that there is some protection, but that there is not more protection that we actually have in countries with representative democracies.

Government policies toward agriculture are extreme in many countries. We see two patterns:
- low-income countries tend to tax domestic agricultural production, whereas high-income countries tend to subsidize and protect it (the development pattern)
- policies tend to tax exportable agricultural products, especially in developing countries, and to protect import-competing products (the antitrade bias).

We present several measures of the effect of government policies on agricultural incomes: the nominal protection coefficient, the effective rate of protection, and the producer subsidy equivalent.

The development pattern may arise because agricultural producers become a more effective lobby as their numbers decrease with the general development of the country's economy, and because agricultural incomes are more sensitive price movements as more of the agricultural output is marketed rather than consumed on the farm. The antitrade bias in developing countries probably arises from government efforts to raise revenues by taxing both imports and exports.

In developed countries most policies are designed to increase farmers' incomes. A common policy is a price support to lift the market price above its free-trade level. This policy must be combined with some kind of restriction on imports. The government may also provide a price support for an exportable product, in which case the government will often effectively subsidize exports to unload the excess domestic production caused by the price support. A price support that is high enough can switch an importable product into an export product, again with the help of export subsidies to unload the excess domestic production.

Many governments claim that they use price supports and other assistance to domestic agriculture to assure food security—reliable supplies. But actual policies often are not consistent with this goal. Economic analysis indicates that import protection is not the best route to food security, except in the unlikely case that the country is threatened by prolonged embargo by a hostile power, and that building domestic food production capability is slow. In other cases, building stockpiles is the better form of insurance.

The agricultural provisions of the Uruguay Round agreement are an effort to make agricultural policy less different. Governments are converting all quotas and other NTBs into tariffs, and developed countries are reducing export and domestic subsidies to agriculture. The actual amount of liberalization is small, but the changes may set the stage for future negotiations to liberalize more.

Tips

Some instructors find the entire chapter to be a good vehicle for discussing the political economy of trade barriers, using agriculture as a major case study. Other instructors may prefer to use only part of the chapter. Here are some suggestions:

- the general political economy of trade policy, using the first part of the chapter (this material can be assigned to accompany Chapter 8 or 9).
- government policies toward agriculture and agricultural trade, omitting the first part of the chapter.
- the political economy of trade barriers and agricultural policy, using the major sections "What Explains Our Trade Barriers in General?" and "The Protection and Taxation of Agriculture."

Suggested answers to questions and problems

(in the textbook)

2.   The free-rider problem is the incentive that each individual has not to contribute to a common endeavor, hoping that others will contribute and the individual will get the benefits of the endeavor without bearing any of the costs. For the political process of trade policy, the free-rider problem can affect how well organized and effective the lobbying groups for and against protection are. Groups like household consumers who are hurt by protection are often ineffective politically. Most household consumers do not become active politically, because of the free-rider problem (or for other reasons). As a result, inefficient import protection policies are adopted.

6.   The nominal protection coefficient is the ratio of the price received by domestic producers to the world price of the same product. If it is greater than one, the product is protected by the government, and if it is less than one, the product is effectively taxed. It does not consider other effects of government policies on farmers' incomes, including direct income subsidies or the effects of government policies on the prices of inputs into agricultural production (or the prices of other things that farm households buy).

8. a.   Both the development pattern and the antitrade bias indicate that the country's government is likely to tax the exportable agricultural products. The development pattern indicates that the country's government is likely to tax domestic production of import-competing agricultural products, and the antitrade bias indicates that it is likely to tax imports of these products as well.

   b.   The development pattern and the antitrade bias both indicate that the country's government is likely to subsidize and protect its agricultural production against imports. All of this country's domestic agricultural production would be import-competing with free trade.

10. a.   The government could offer production subsidies to wheat and rice farmers, and also subsidize imports of wheat and rice (with the import subsidy at a lesser rate per unit than the production subsidy rate).

    b.   We'll examine the Nigerian market for wheat, assuming that Nigeria is small country. The analysis for rice is similar. With free trade at the world price P_0, Nigeria produces S_0 and consumes D_0. The import subsidy reduces the domestic price to P_1. This is the price consumers pay, so they increase consumption to D_1. Domestic producers receive both the

68

market price P_1 and the production subsidy, so they effectively receive the price P_2. In response they increase production to S_1. Imports are $(D_1 - S_1)$. In comparison with free trade, domestic producer surplus increases by area a, and domestic consumer surplus increases by area $(c + e + f + g + h)$. The cost to the government of the import subsidy is area $(g + h + j)$, and government cost of the production subsidy is area $(a + b + c + e + f)$. The welfare cost of the set of subsidies is areas b and j. These are two types of deadweight loss—the inefficiency of high-cost domestic production (area b), and the inefficiency of excessive domestic consumption (area j). The extra consumption is inefficient because the cost to country of importing the extra units consumed is P_0, but consumers value these units at lesser amounts shown by the height of the demand curve.

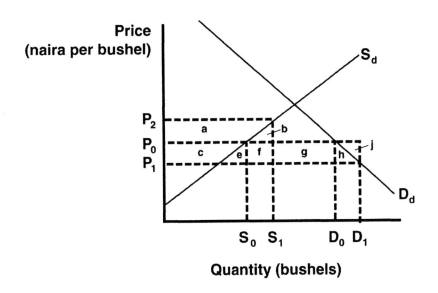

69

Chapter 15

Payments among Nations

Overview

This chapter begins the discussion of international finance and macroeconomics—the subject of Parts III and IV of the book. Its major purpose is to show how the balance of payments arises from various international transactions and how the different balances (or sub-balances) can be interpreted. It also presents the international investment position.

A country's balance of payments records all economic transactions between the residents of the country and residents of the rest of the world. Each transaction or exchange results in two opposite flows of value. By convention, a credit or positive item is the flow for which the country is paid—it sets up a claim on the foreign resident, so that funds (or "money") flow into the country. A debit or negative item is the flow that the country must pay for—it sets up a foreign claim on a resident of the country, so that funds (or "money") flow out of the country. Each transaction has both a credit and a debit item—double-entry bookkeeping—at least once we create a fictional "goodwill" item for things that are given away (unilateral or unrequited transfers). Therefore, if we add up all items for the country's balance of payments, it must add up to zero. What we find interesting about the balance of payments is not that it must completely add up to zero, but rather how it does so. What are the values of different categories of items?

Typically, the first categories we examine are items that are international flows of goods (or merchandise), services, income, and gifts—the current account. Services include flows of transportation, financial services, education, consulting, and so forth. Income includes flows of payments such as interest, dividends, and profits. In addition to the full current account balance, we can also examine the goods and services balance.

The (private) capital account includes items that are nonofficial international flows of financial assets. Capital inflows are credit items—capital or funds flow into the country as the country "exports" financial assets (by increasing liabilities to foreigners or decreasing assets previously obtained from foreigners). Capital outflows are debit items—capital or funds flow out of the country as the country "imports" financial assets (by increasing the country's assets obtained from foreigners or decreasing its liabilities to foreigners). Direct investments are international capital flows between units of a company located in different countries (Chapter 27 has a detailed discussion of direct foreign investment and multinational firms). If the investor does not have management control, international investments in stocks and bonds are usually called portfolio investments. International loans and bank deposits are other capital flows included in the capital account.

The third and final major part of the country's balance of payments records official international flows of financial assets that serve as official international reserves. The country's monetary authority (usually, its central bank) undertakes these transactions. Official international reserves include financial assets denominated in readily accepted foreign currencies, the country's holdings of Special Drawing Rights (SDRs), the country's reserve position at the International Monetary Fund (IMF), and gold.

If all items are recorded correctly, the sum of all of these items equal zero. In practice, they are not and do not, so that a line called "statistical discrepancy" is added to make the accounts add to zero. It represents the net of many items that are mismeasured or missed (net errors and omissions).

The current account balance (CA) has several meanings. First, it is approximately equal to the difference (X - M) between the value of the country's exports of goods and services and the value of its imports of goods and services. Second, it equals the value of the country's net flow (I_f) of foreign investments (both private and official). Third, it is difference between national saving and domestic real investment (S - I_d). Fourth, it is the difference between domestic production of goods and services and national expenditures on goods and services (Y - E). The text shows how the current account and goods and services balances have changed over time for four countries— the United States, Canada, Japan, and Mexico.

The overall balance should indicate whether a country's balance of payments has achieved an overall pattern that is sustainable over time. While there is no perfect indicator of overall balance, we often examine the country's official settlements balance (B), which is the sum (CA + KA) of the current account balance and the private capital account balance (including the statistical discrepancy). The official settlements balance also equals the (negative of the) official reserves balance (OR). Most of the official reserves flows indicate official intervention by the monetary authorities in the foreign exchange market.

The international investment position is a statement of the stocks of a country's foreign assets and foreign liabilities at a point in time. The text shows that the United States has changed from being an international debtor to creditor and back to a debtor during the past century.

Tips

A key decision faced by the instructor is whether or not to cover the posting of transactions to the credit and debit items. Although the text presents some examples of this process, it is not necessary to cover it in class. Students generally can grasp the meaning of the balance of payments by focusing on the various lines (showing types of items) and balances—as long as the students also see that it is double-entry bookkeeping so that all items must add up to zero.

A good source of up-to-date information on many countries is the *Balance of Payments Yearbook* published by the International Monetary Fund. The summary table for one country can be used for class presentation and discussion. The format for the current account is similar to the presentation used in the text. However, the IMF now uses the term "Financial Account" to refer to what is usually called the capital account. (And, to add to the confusion, the IMF has a small set of items like capital transfers that it calls the "Capital Account.") In addition, the official reserves account shown by the IMF includes only changes in official reserve assets held by the country's own central bank or monetary authority. The omission of changes in foreign official holdings of the country's liabilities is not a major issue for most countries, but it is important for a country like the United States, whose own liabilities are held in large amounts by foreign central banks.

Suggested answers to questions and problems

(in the textbook)

2.   Disagree, at least as a general statement. One meaning of a current account surplus is that the country is exporting more goods and services than it is importing. One might easily judge that this is not good—the country is producing goods and services that are exported, but the country is not at the same time getting the imports of goods and services that would allow it do more consumption and domestic investment. In this way a current account deficit might be considered good—the extra imports allow the country to consume and invest domestically more than the value of its current production. Another meaning of a current account surplus is that the country is engaging in foreign financial investment—it is building up its claims on foreigners, and this adds to national wealth. This sounds good, but as noted above it comes at the cost of foregoing current domestic expenditures. A current account deficit is the country running down its claims on foreigners or increasing its indebtedness to foreigners. This sounds bad, but it comes with the benefit of higher levels of current domestic expenditure. Different countries at different times may weigh the balance of these costs and benefits differently, so that we cannot simply say that a current account surplus is better than a current account deficit.

4.   Disagree. If the country has a surplus (a positive value) for its official settlements balance, then the value for its official reserves balance must be a negative value of the same amount (so that the two add to zero). A negative value for this asset item means that funds are flowing out in order for the country to acquire more of these kinds of assets. Thus, the country is increasing its holdings of official reserve assets.

6.   Item e is a transaction in which foreign official holdings of U.S. assets increase. This is a positive (credit) item for official reserve assets and a negative (debit) item for private capital flows as the U.S. bank acquires DM bank deposits. The debit item contributes to a U.S. deficit in the official settlements balance (while the credit item is recorded "below the line," permitting the official settlements balance to be in deficit). All other transactions involve debit and credit items both of which are included in the official settlements balance, so that they do not directly contribute to a deficit (or surplus) in the official settlements balance.

8. a.   Merchandise trade balance: $330 - 198 = $132
          Goods and services balance: $330 - 198 + 196 - 204 = $124
          Current account balance: $330 - 198 + 196 - 204 + 3 - 8 = $119
          Official settlements balance: $330 - 198 + 196 - 204 + 3 - 8 + 102 - 202 + 4 = $23
   b.   Change in official reserve assets (net) = - official settlements balance = -$23.
          The country is increasing its net holdings of official reserve assets.

10. a.   International investment position (billions): $30 + 20 + 15 - 40 - 25 = $0.

The country is neither an international creditor nor a debtor. Its holding of international assets equals its liabilities to foreigners.

b. A current account surplus permits the country to add to its net claims on foreigners. For this reason the country's international investment position will become a positive value. The flow increase in net foreign assets results in the stock of net foreign assets becoming positive.

Chapter 16

The Foreign Exchange Market

Overview

The purpose of this chapter is to present the foreign exchange market and exchange rates, with an emphasis on spot exchange rates. Foreign exchange is the act of trading different countries' moneys. An exchange rate is the price of one money in terms of another. The spot exchange rate is the price for "immediate" exchange. The forward exchange rate is the price agreed to today for exchanges that will take place in the future. An exchange rate is confusing because there is no natural way to quote the price. The text adopts the convention of quoting the rate as the price of foreign currency—units of the home currency per unit of foreign currency. (The currency that is being priced by the rate is in the denominator.)

At the center of the foreign exchange market are a group of banks that use telecommunications and computers to conduct trades with their customers (the retail part of the market) and with each other (the interbank part of the market). Most foreign exchange trades are conducted by exchanging ownership of demand deposits denominated in different currencies.

We can picture the foreign exchange market by using demand and supply curves. Exports of goods and services and capital outflows (as well as income payments to foreigners) create a demand for foreign currency, as payments for these items typically require that at some point in the payment process the home currency is exchanged for the foreign currency to pay for the items that the home residents are buying. Imports of goods and services and capital inflows (as well as income received from foreign sources) create a supply of foreign currency, as payments for these items typically require that at some point in the payment process the foreign currency is exchanged for the home currency to pay for the items that the foreign residents are buying.

The text explains the downward slope of the demand curve for foreign currency through changes in the dollar price of products that the home country might buy from the foreign country, as the going spot exchange rate changes. (The text assumes that the supply curve slopes upward, without much discussion at this point. The details of how values of exports and imports respond to changes in the exchange rate are deferred until the end of Chapter 22.)

In a floating exchange rate system without intervention by monetary authorities, the equilibrium is at the intersection of the demand and supply curves, where the curves show all private (or nonofficial) demand and supply. The floating exchange rate changes as demand and supply curves shift over time. In a fixed exchange rate system, government officials declare that the exchange rate should be a certain level, usually within a small band around a par value. We can still use demand and supply to analyze this system. If the equilibrium rate that the market would set on its own (shown by the intersection of the private or nonofficial demand and supply curves) is outside of this band, then the officials must do something to prevent the actual rate from moving outside of the band. We focus on defense through official intervention—the officials must buy or sell foreign currency (in exchange for domestic currency) to keep the exchange rate within (or at the edge) of the band. This can be pictured as filling the gap between nonofficial supply and demand at the support-point exchange rate. (The intervention could also be pictured as shifting the overall supply or demand curve—each overall curve would include both nonofficial and official supply or demand—so that the new intersection occurs at the support point.)

The chapter concludes by introducing the two different kinds of arbitrage that can occur using the spot foreign exchange market. The simpler form is arbitrage of the same exchange rate between two locations. This arbitrage assures that, at a particular time, the same exchange rate is essentially the same value in different locations (at least within a small range that reflects transactions costs). The more complicated form is triangular arbitrage—profiting from misalignments among two exchange rates against a common currency (usually the dollar, which is the vehicle currency in the market) and the cross-rate between the other two currencies (for instance, pounds and Swiss francs). This type of arbitrage assures that the cross-rate essentially equals the ratio of the other two exchange rates.

Tips

Footnote 3 explains the conventions used by traders to quote exchange rates. It also notes that we ignore the distinction between bid and ask prices in out general discussion.

This chapter is intended to introduce key features of the foreign exchange market and present the basic demand-supply analysis of spot exchange rates. A key goal is to get students thinking about exchange rates as prices, about demand-supply pressures on exchange rates, and about the opportunity for arbitrage using the foreign exchange market. At the same time students should be assured that many of the topics, including what shifts the nonofficial supply and demand curves, as well as government policies toward the foreign exchange market, will be taken up in more depth as we cover the next four chapters of this Part.

We choose to picture the foreign exchange market using a standard demand and supply graph in which the demand curve slopes downward and the supply curve slopes upward. Of course, this is most consistent with discussions that focus on flow demand and supply (an approach that is regaining some prominence in current research on exchange rates). Students seem to have success grasping this approach, as it builds on their previous economics learning. The examples in the text focus on the shape of and shifts in the demand curve, so that the instructor may choose to present class discussion using stocks of money supply and demand, and this will appear to be reasonably consistent with the text (except that the supply curve used in class may be vertical). Also, as noted in the overview, we choose not to go into details at this point about the slope of the supply curve. This detailed discussion tends to confuse some students and it diverts them from the basic points about using demand-supply logic. Footnote 6 notes that the actual slope of the supply curve is not clear-cut.

The box "Birth of a Currency" discusses the creation of the euro in 1999. The process of European Monetary Union is discussed in more depth in Chapters 20 and 24.

Suggested answers to questions and problems
(in the textbook)

2. *Exports of merchandise and services* result in supply of foreign currency in the foreign exchange market. Domestic sellers often want to be paid using domestic currency, while the foreign buyers want to pay in their currency. In the process of paying for these exports, foreign currency is exchanged for domestic currency, creating supply of foreign currency. *International capital inflows* result in a supply of foreign currency in the foreign exchange market. In making investments in domestic financial assets, foreign investors often start with foreign currency and must exchange it for domestic currency before they can buy the domestic assets. The exchange creates a supply of foreign currency. Sales of foreign financial assets that the country's residents had previously acquired, and borrowing from foreigners by this country's residents are other forms of capital inflow that can create supply of foreign currency.

4. The U.S. firm obtains a quotation from its bank on the spot exchange rate for buying yen with dollars. If the rate is acceptable, the firm instructs its bank that it wants to use dollars from its dollar checking account to buy 1 million yen at this spot exchange rate. It also instructs its bank to send the yen to the bank account of the Japanese firm. To carry out this instruction, the U.S. bank instructs its correspondent bank in Japan to take 1 million yen from its account at the correspondent bank and transfer the yen to the bank account of the Japanese firm. (The U.S. bank could also use yen at its own branch if it has a branch in Japan.)

6. The trader would seek out the best quoted spot rate for buying euros with dollars, either through direct contact with traders at other banks or by using the services of a foreign exchange broker. The trader would use the best rate to buy euro spot. Sometime in the next hour or so (or, typically at least by the end of the day), the trader will enter the interbank market again, to obtain the best quoted spot rate for selling euros for dollars. The trader will use the best spot rate to sell her previously acquired euros. If the spot value of the euro has risen during this short time, the trader makes a profit.

8. a. The cross rate between the yen and the krone is too high (the yen value of the krone is too high) relative to the dollar-foreign currency exchange rates. Thus, in a profitable triangular arbitrage, you want to sell kroner at the high cross rate. The arbitrage will be: Use dollars to buy kroner at $0.20/krone, use these kroner to buy yen at 25 yen/krone, and use the yen to buy dollars at $0.01/yen. For each dollar that you sell initially, you can obtain 5 kroner, these 5 kroner can obtain 125 yen, and the 125 yen can obtain $1.25. The arbitrage profit for each dollar is therefore 25 cents.
   b. Selling kroner to buy yen puts downward pressure on the cross rate (the yen price of krone). The value of the cross rate must fall to 20 (=0.20/0.01) yen/krone to eliminate the opportunity for triangular arbitrage.

10. a. The increase in supply of Swiss francs puts downward pressure on the exchange-rate value ($/SFr) of the franc. The monetary authorities must intervene to defend the fixed exchange rate by buying SFr and selling dollars.

b. The increase in supply of francs puts downward pressure on the exchange-rate value ($/SFr) of the franc. The monetary authorities must intervene to defend the fixed exchange rate by buying SFr and selling dollars.
c. The increase in supply of francs puts downward pressure on the exchange-rate value ($/SFr) of the franc. The monetary authorities must intervene to defend the fixed exchange rate by buying SFr and selling dollars.
d. The decrease in demand for francs puts downward pressure on the exchange-rate value ($/SFr) of the franc. The monetary authorities must intervene to defend the fixed exchange rate by buying SFr and selling dollars.

Chapter 17

Forward Exchange

Overview

This chapter is intended to present the uses of forward foreign exchange rates and the returns and risks of international financial investments, both covered and uncovered. It begins by noting that in many situations people or organizations are exposed to exchange rate risk, because the value of the individual's income, wealth, or net worth changes when exchange rates change unexpectedly in the future. A net asset position in the foreign currency is called a long position; a net liability position is called a short position. Some individuals want to reduce their risk exposure by hedging—an action to reduce a net asset or net liability position in a foreign currency. Other individuals may actually want to take on risk exposure in order to profit from exchange rate changes, by speculating—an action to take on a net asset or net liability position in a foreign currency.

A forward foreign exchange contract is an agreement to exchange a certain amount of one currency for a certain amount of another currency on some date in the future, with the amounts based on the price (forward exchange rate) set when the contract is entered. Because the forward exchange contract establishes a position in foreign currency, it can be used to hedge or to speculate. A key conclusion from the use of forward foreign exchange contracts to speculate is that the pressures on the supply and demand of forward foreign exchange should drive the forward exchange rate to equal the average expected value of the future spot exchange rate. (Also, a forward foreign exchange contract is a kind of derivative contract based on exchange rates. A box in the text discusses other foreign-exchange contracts—currency futures, options, and swaps.)

International financial investment has grown rapidly in recent decades. Decisions about international investments depend on both returns and risks. The text focuses on calculating returns. It also discusses risks, including mention of risk as a portfolio issue (although a full treatment of international portfolio diversification is not provided).

An investor who calculates her wealth and returns in her home currency can easily calculate returns on investments denominated in her own currency. Investments in foreign currency-denominated assets are a bit more complicated. She must first convert her own currency into the foreign currency at the spot exchange rate. Then she uses this foreign currency to buy the foreign asset, and earns returns in foreign currency. Then, she must convert this foreign currency in the future back into her own currency (either actually or simply to determine the value of her wealth). She could contract now for the future currency conversion using a forward exchange contract, in which case she has a covered international investment, and she is hedged against exchange rate risk. Or, she can wait until the future and convert currencies at the spot exchange rate that exists at that date in the future, in which case she has an uncovered international investment, and she is exposed to exchange rate risk.

An investor can compare the return on a covered international investment to the return on a home investment using the covered interest differential (CD). The exact expression is $CD = (1 + i_f) \cdot r_f / r_s - (1 + i)$, where the i's are the foreign (subscript f) and domestic interest rates and the r's are the forward (subscript f) and spot (subscript s) exchange rates. A useful approximation is $CD = F + (i_f - i)$, where F is the forward premium (discount if negative) on the foreign currency. If CD is not zero (or within a small range close to zero, determined by transactions costs), then international investors can engage in covered interest arbitrage—buying a country's currency spot and selling it forward, while making a net profit from the combination of the interest rate difference and the forward premium or discount. Because covered interest arbitrage is essentially riskless (as long as there is no threat of exchange controls or similar government impediments), this arbitrage should drive the covered differential to be essentially zero—covered interest parity. Covered interest parity links four current market rates together—the forward exchange rate, the spot exchange rate, and the interest rates in the two countries. If one of these rates changes, then at least one other also must change to reestablish covered interest parity.

At the time that an investor makes the investment, he can calculate the return expected on an uncovered international investment using the spot exchange rate that he expects to exist in the future. He can compare this expected return to the return on a home investment using the expected uncovered interest differential (EUD). The exact expression is $EUD = (1 + i_f) \cdot r_s^e / r_s - (1 + i)$, where r_s^e is the expected future spot exchange rate. A useful approximation is that EUD equals the expected rate of appreciation (depreciation if negative) of the foreign currency plus the interest differential $(i_f - i)$. The box on "The World's Greatest Investor" provides a profile of George Soros, who has made (and sometimes lost) billions of dollars with large uncovered or speculative investment positions.

An uncovered international investment is exposed to exchange rate risk. Nonetheless, the investor may still undertake the uncovered investment, because the expected return is high enough to compensate for the risk, or, more subtly, because the uncovered investment may actually reduce the risk of the investor's overall portfolio because of the benefits of diversification of investments. If risk considerations are small, then investors will shift toward investments with higher (expected) returns. Demand-supply pressures on market rates will drive rates to eliminate the return differential, so that the uncovered interest differential is essentially zero—uncovered interest parity.

The final section of the chapter presents some evidence on whether the various parity conditions actually hold. Covered interest parity holds well between currencies of countries whose governments permit free movements of international capital. It is more difficult to test uncovered interest parity, because we cannot observe the expected future spot exchange rate in the market. (If we use the forward rate as an indicator of the expected future spot exchange rate, then we are really just testing covered interest parity.) Indirect tests of covered interest parity suggest that it does not hold as tightly as covered interest parity. While divergences from uncovered interest parity could simply indicate risk premiums to compensate for exposure to exchange rate risk, some studies suggest that the deviations are larger than seem necessary to compensate for such risk. Instead, expectations of future spot exchange rates seem to be biased. Such an apparent bias would not be troubling if market participants are correctly anticipating the probability of a large shift in the exchange rate at some time in the future (even if the rate does not actually change). The apparent bias is troubling if it reflects consistent errors, implying inefficiency in the foreign exchange market.

Tips

In presenting this material, it is useful to build the overall return on a foreign financial investment step-by-step: spot exchange (r_s), invest in the foreign currency-denominated financial asset ($1 + i_f$), and exchange back into home currency (r_f or r_s^e). The lake diagram (Figure 17.1) pictures this process for covered investments and permits movements in any direction. A comparable diagram for uncovered investments could be provided to the class, in which r_f is replaced by r_s^e (for analysis ex ante).

This points out a broader goal of the style of presentation used in the text. We strive to show how similar covered and uncovered investments are (as well as the specific ways in which they are different). The focus on the similarities allows students to transfer insights from the discussion of covered investments to their analysis of uncovered investments.

An excellent device for getting students to plunge into the foreign exchange market and to gain insights into exchange rate risk and future spot exchange rates is to ask them to predict what exchange rates (and perhaps the price of gold) will be one or three months in the future. (The time period of one or three months is desirable because newspapers like the *Wall Street Journal* publish the 30-day and 90-day forward exchange rates. You might even hand out the current full table to students as part of the "assignment.") This exercise can be submitted at the beginning of the term, at the beginning of the material on international finance (if this is not the beginning of the term), or at the conclusion of the presentation of the material in this Chapter 17. If desirable, prizes can be offered to the best guessers, either rate-by-rate or overall (using lowest average absolute percentage errors). The sample assignment on the accompanying page offers one version of this exercise. After all guesses are submitted, the instructor could provide graphs showing the distributions of guesses by the class. In addition, the "debriefing" at the conclusion of the contest could include charts of how the rates moved day-by-day during the contest time period, with indications of the initial forward rate, the class median guess, and the instructor's guess.

Suggested answers to questions and problems
(in the textbook)

2. You will need data on four market rates: The current interest rate (or yield) on bonds issued by the U.S. government that mature in one year, the current interest rate (or yield) on bonds issued by the British government that mature in one year, the current spot exchange rate between the dollar and pound, and the current one-year forward exchange rate between the dollar and pound. Do these rates result in a covered interest differential that is very close to zero?

4. a. The U.S. firm has an asset position in yen—it has a long position in yen. To hedge its exposure to exchange rate risk, the firm should enter into a forward exchange contract

now in which the firm commits to sell yen and receive dollars at the current forward rate. The contract amounts are to sell 1 million yen and receive $9,000, both in 60 days.

b. The student has an asset position in yen—a long position in yen. To hedge the exposure to exchange rate risk, the student should enter into a forward exchange contract now in which the student commits to sell yen and receive dollars at the current forward rate. The contract amounts are to sell 10 million yen and receive $90,000, both in 60 days.

c. The U.S. firm has an liability position in yen—a short position in yen. To hedge its exposure to exchange rate risk, the firm should enter into a forward exchange contract now in which the firm commits to sell dollars and receive yen at the current forward rate. The contract amounts are to sell $900,000 and receive 100 million yen, both in 60 days.

6. Relative to your expected spot value of the euro in 90 days ($1.22/euro), the current forward rate of the euro ($1.18/euro) is low—the forward value of the euro is relatively low. Using the principle of "buy low, sell high," you can speculate by entering into a forward contract now to buy euros at $1.18/euro. If you are correct in your expectation, then in 90 days you will be able to immediately resell those euros for $1.22/euro, pocketing a profit of $0.04 for each euro that you bought forward. If many people speculate in this way, then massive purchases now of euros forward (increasing the demand for euros forward) will tend to drive up the forward value of the euro, toward a current forward rate of $1.22/euro.

8. a. The Swiss franc is at a forward premium. Its current forward value ($0.505/SFr) is greater than its current spot value ($0.500/SFr).

b. The covered interest differential "in favor of Switzerland" is $((1 + 0.005) \cdot (0.505) / 0.500) - (1 + 0.01) = 0.005$. (Note that the interest rate used must match the time period of the investment.) There is a covered interest differential of 0.5% for 30 days (6 percent at an annual rate). The U.S. investor can make a higher return, covered against exchange rate risk, by investing in SFr-denominated bonds, so presumably the investor should make this covered investment. Although the interest rate on SFr-denominated bonds is lower than the interest rate on dollar-denominated bonds, the forward premium on the franc is larger than this difference, so that the covered investment is a good idea.

c. The lack of demand for dollar-denominated bonds (or the supply of these bonds as investors sell them in order to shift into SFr-denominated bonds) puts downward pressure on the prices of U.S. bonds—upward pressure on U.S. interest rates. The extra demand for the franc in the spot exchange market (as investors buy SFr in order to buy SFr-denominated bonds) puts upward pressure on the spot exchange rate. The extra demand for SFr-denominated bonds puts upward pressure on the prices of Swiss bonds—downward pressure on Swiss interest rates. The extra supply of francs in the forward market (as U.S. investors cover their SFr investments back into dollars) puts downward pressure on the forward exchange rate. If the only rate that changes is the forward exchange rate, this rate must fall to about $0.5025/SFr. With this forward rate and the other initial rates, the covered interest differential is close to zero.

10. In testing covered interest parity, all of the interest rates and exchange rates that are needed to calculate the covered interest differential are rates that can observed in the bond and foreign exchange markets. Determining whether the covered interest differential is

about zero (covered interest parity) is then straightforward (although some more subtle issues regarding timing of transactions may also need to be addressed). In order to test uncovered interest parity, we need to know not only three rates—two interest rates and the current spot exchange rate—that can be observed in the market, but also one rate—the expected future spot exchange rate—that is not observed in any market. The tester then needs a way to find out about investors' expectations. One way is to ask them, using a survey, but they may not say exactly what they really think. Another way is to examine the actual uncovered interest differential after we know what the future spot exchange rate actually turns out to be, and see whether the statistical characteristics of the actual uncovered differential are consistent with an expected uncovered differential of about zero (uncovered interest parity).

Sample assignment

University of California—Davis
Economics 160B
International Macroeconomics

Prof. Lindert
Spring 1999

Speculate!!

What will the yen, the Mexican peso, the pound sterling, the euro, and gold be worth a month from now? Show your financial genius by filling in your forecasts below. Return this form to lecture this Thursday, April 8.

For the purposes of this exercise, "a month from now" means the Wall Street Journal spot quotes for 4:00 PM Eastern time in New York on Thursday, May 6. The winning guesses will be announced in class on Tuesday, May 11. If you are the winner of any of these categories, yours is the satisfaction of knowing that you could have made a bundle if your guess had been backed by millions of dollars. There is an additional incentive: the best guessers in each category are my guests for a free Winner Dinner on May 25 at 6:00 PM. In addition, there is a special prize for the individual with the very best set of forecasts (smallest average percentage error, with percentage errors calculated against the final actual values).

To guide your choice, here are some recent data on exchange rates and gold prices:

	A month ago	Yesterday
British pound sterling	$1.6067	$1.5995
ditto, 30-day forward	$1.6059	$1.5990
Japanese yen	$0.008145	$0.008207
ditto, 30-day forward	$0.008178	$0.008239
Mexican peso, floating rate	$0.1011	$0.1056
Euro	$1.0833	$1.0710
ditto, 30-day forward	$1.0850	$1.0725
Gold	$287.90	$280.55 (April 1)

(ballot on the next page)

Sterling: I predict that the spot price of the British pound in New York, 4:00 Eastern time, May 6 will be, in dollars with four decimal places:

$_ . _ _ _ _

Yen: I predict that the spot price of Japanese yen, same time and place, will be, with six decimal places:

$_ . _ _ _ _ _ _

Peso: I predict that the spot price of the Mexican peso, same time and place, will be, with four decimal places:

$_ . _ _ _ _

Euro: I predict that the spot price of the euro, same time and place, will be, with four decimal places:

$_ . _ _ _ _

Gold: I predict that the London PM fixing price of gold, same date, will be, in dollars and cents per ounce:

$_ _ _ . _ _

My name

_____

Chapter 18

What Determines Exchange Rates in the Long Run?

Overview

Since the general shift to floating exchange rates in the early 1970s, exchange rates between the U.S. dollar and other major currencies have been variable or volatile. The charts at the beginning of the chapter suggest three types of variability. First, there are long-term trends in which some currencies tend to appreciate against the dollar, and other tend to depreciate. Second, there are medium-term trends which are sometimes counter to the longer trends. Third, there is a substantial variability during the short run.

This chapter focuses on what we know about the long trends. Our understanding of exchange rates in the long run is based on the purchasing power parity (PPP) hypothesis— products should have similar prices in all countries when the prices are measured in the same currency, at least in the long run when a full market equilibrium is established. According to PPP, $P = r_s \cdot P_f$ (or $r_s = P/P_f$), where the P's are prices (measured in local currencies) in the home and foreign countries.

The evidence generally indicates the following about PPP. First, PPP predicts well at the level of one heavily traded commodity (like wheat or gold). This version is sometimes called the law of one price. Second, PPP predicts only moderately well at the level of all traded products. Third, PPP predicts least well at the level of all products in the economy. Finally, and perhaps most importantly, PPP predicts better over the long run than in the short run. The text also presents recent evidence on the version of PPP (sometimes called relative PPP) that examines the relationship between the inflation rates (rates of change of product prices) in different countries and the rates of the change of the exchange rate between the countries' currencies. A relationship consistent with PPP is clear—low-inflation countries tend to have appreciating currencies and high inflation countries tend to have depreciating currencies. In addition, examination of the dollar-mark and dollar-yen exchange rates shows that there is a tendency to follow PPP in the long run, but that there are also substantial deviations from PPP in the short run.

If exchange rates follow national price levels in the long run, what determines national price levels in the long run? In the long run the national money supply (or its growth rate) determines the national price level (or the national inflation rate), through the equilibrium between money supply and money demand. In the text we use the demand for money that follows the quantity theory of money, in order to draw out the relationships in the most direct manner possible. Money is held to facilitate transactions, so that money demand is based on the annual turnover of transactions that require money, and this turnover is proxied by the level of (nominal) domestic product ($P \cdot Y$, where Y is real GDP). The quantity theory then says that, for each country, $M^s = k \cdot P \cdot Y$, where M^s is the national money supply, which is controlled by national monetary policy, and k is a behavioral parameter.

Combining PPP and the quantity theory equations for two countries, we obtain a basis for the monetary approach to explaining or predicting exchange rates in the long run: $r_s = P/P_f = (M^s/M^s_f) \cdot (k_f/k) \cdot (Y_f/Y)$. If the ratio of the k's is steady, then the exchange rate will change over the long run as the money supplies change and as real GDPs grow, with elasticities of one. Other things equal, in the long run a lower level (or slower growth over time) of a country's money supply, or a higher level (or faster growth) of its real GDP, tend to result in a higher value (an appreciation over time) of the country's currency, because each implies a lower level (or slower rate of increase) in the country's price level.

The box on "Tracking the Exchange Rate Value of a Currency" introduces some concepts and distinctions that are useful in examining exchange rates. Nominal bilateral exchange rates are simply the standard rates quoted in the foreign exchange market. The nominal effective exchange rate is an index that tracks the weighted-average nominal value of a county's currency. Deviations from PPP can be measured using the real exchange rate, which can be measured as an index between two currencies (bilateral) or as a weighted average index relative to a number of other currencies (effective). If PPP holds in the long run, then the real exchange rate tends to return to its "normal" value (e.g., 100).

Tips

We choose not to elaborate on the money demand function at this time in the text. In Part IV we add the interest rate as a determinant of money demand, but for the long-run analysis emphasized here it does not seem necessary. An instructor could incorporate the interest rate as a determinant of money demand by discussing what might determine the k value in the quantity equation.

Students benefit from the application of the concepts from Chapters 15-18 to the real world. You may want to consider an assignment like the one that Pugel and others at New York University have used successfully. It asks students to apply the concepts to a country other than the United States. The sample assignment on the accompanying pages shows one version, in which students worked in groups, but the students could instead be asked to work individually. (In addition, each group used the same country that it had used for a previous assignment in the course.) If you use a comparable assignment, it can be distributed about the time that you finish covering the material from Chapter 18 (especially PPP and real exchange rates).

Appendix F shows that interest rate parities and purchasing power parity can be combined. This combination provides additional insights, including the proposition of the equality of real interest rates across countries.

Suggested answers to questions and problems

(in the text)

2.   According to PPP, the exchange rate value of the DM (relative to the dollar) has risen since the early 1970s because Germany has experienced less inflation than has the United States—the product price level has risen less in Germany since the early 1970s than it has risen in the United States. According to the monetary approach, the German price level has not risen as much because the German money supply has increased less than the

money supply has increased in the United States, relative to the growth rates of real domestic production in the two countries. The British pound is the opposite case—more inflation in Britain than in the United States, and higher money growth in Britain.

4.   Disagree. If we use the monetary approach to evaluate this proposition, then it is not necessarily true. Even if the ks (the behavioral proportions) are constant, the monetary approach also says that the growth rates of real domestic products matter. Even if the growth rates of the money supplies are the same, the country that has the higher growth rate of real product will have a lower rate of price inflation, so that this country will have an appreciating currency.

6.   You would be bullish on the New Zealand currency's exchange-rate value. If New Zealand maintains an inflation rate that is very close to zero, then it will be one of the lowest-inflation countries in the world. According to PPP, a low-inflation country tends to have an appreciating currency in the long run, relative to the currencies of other countries with higher inflation rates.

8. a.   Because the growth rate of the domestic money supply (M^s) is two percentage points higher than it was previously, the monetary approach indicates that the exchange rate value (r_s) of the foreign currency will be higher than it otherwise would be—that is, the exchange rate value of the country's currency will be lower. Specifically, the foreign currency will appreciate by two percentage points more per year, or depreciate by two percentage points less. That is, the domestic currency will depreciate by two percentage points more per year, or appreciate by two percentage points less.

   b.   The faster growth of the country's money supply eventually leads to a faster rate of inflation of the domestic price level (P). Specifically, the inflation rate will be two percentage points higher than it otherwise would be. According to PPP, a faster rate of increase in the domestic price level (P) leads to a higher exchange rate value for the foreign currency.

10. a. For the United States in 1975, $20,000 = k \cdot 100 \cdot 800$, or $k = 0.25$.
        For Pugelovia in 1975, $10,000 = k \cdot 100 \cdot 200$, or $k = 0.5$.

   b.   For the United States, the quantity theory of money with a constant k means that the quantity equation with $k = 0.25$ should hold in 2000: $65,000 = 0.25 \cdot 260 \cdot 1,000$. It does. Because the quantity equation holds for both years with the same k, the change in the price level from 1975 to 2000 is consistent with the quantity theory of money with a constant k. Similarly, for Pugelovia, the quantity equation with $k = 0.5$ should hold for 2000, and it does ($58,500 = 0.5 \cdot 390 \cdot 300$).

Sample assignment

NEW YORK UNIVERSITY
Stern School of Business

C45.0001 Economics of International Business
Prof. T. Pugel
Spring 1999

Country Assignment #2

This group assignment is due on Wednesday, April 28, 1999. **NO LATE PAPERS WILL BE ACCEPTED.**

The text of your group's answers to the assignment should be typed single-spaced, with an extra space between each paragraph. The text must be limited to a maximum of three pages. You may also attach additional tables and charts to this three pages of text, if these tables and charts are of direct importance to your text discussion.

The group members are not to discuss this assignment with anyone else who is not in the group (except for consulting reference librarians in order to locate materials). The group may utilize any published materials -- you are not limited to the sources noted in the assignment description below.

The Assignment

1. What have been the trends in the <u>nominal exchange rate</u> values (annual averages) of your country's currency since <u>1980</u>, relative to the U.S. dollar? Relative to the U.S. dollar, has the currency of your country tended to appreciate or to depreciate?

    Most likely source of data (for this part and for the next part): IMF, <u>International Financial Statistics (IFS) Yearbook</u>, or the related monthly issues of the <u>IFS</u>. Use period-average annual values of exchange rates. (You need to make sure that you are using the same monetary units for the exchange rate values for your country during the entire period—for some countries you must make adjustments according to information in the source.)

2. Calculate and report the <u>real exchange rate</u> values (annual averages) of your country's currency since <u>1980</u>, relative to the U.S. dollar. In your calculations, use the wholesale (or producer or industrial or home goods) price index (or a similar price index—line 63 of the IFS) if this is available for your country. If this is not available, use the consumer price index or the GDP deflator. (If none of these are available, please see me to discuss any other alternatives). In reporting the values of these real exchange rates, use a base year of 1980=100. [Please attach an appendix in which the methods of calculating the real exchange rates are documented.]

Relative to the base year of 1980, what do these values of the real exchange rate imply for your country's international price competitiveness for various times during this period?

(Again, for the variables that you use in your calculations, you will need to make sure that you are using consistent units for each variable over the entire time period.)

3. You are a U.S. investor who calculates your income and wealth in U.S. dollars. Currently you have no assets or liabilities denominated in the currency of your assignment country. You are considering an uncovered international financial investment into a short-term or medium-term debt security (or bank deposit) denominated in the local currency, rather than investing in a comparable U.S.-dollar debt security. The debt security (or deposit) is one that is issued by a high-quality domestic organization from your assignment country (e.g., the national government, a domestic bank, or a high-grade corporate issuer), and the debt security (or deposit) is one that matures in one to two years (or one that is as close to this maturity as possible). You will need to find a source that provides the current (or very recent) yield (interest rate) on an appropriate debt security for your assignment country.

Discuss the ingredients that go into the analysis of whether or not to make this uncovered international financial investment. What factors suggest that the uncovered international investment is attractive? What factors suggest that the uncovered international investment is unattractive? What factors are approximately neutral? In your answer to this part, use concepts and tools from the course that are relevant to the analysis. Also, as one part of your answer, discuss how your analysis of the real exchange rate (part 2 of this assignment) is relevant to your evaluation of the uncovered international investment.

In addition to the data shown in the International Financial Statistics or various national data sources, you might use sources (among other possibilities) such as:

> Listings of yields in the Financial Times or Wall Street Journal.
> Economist Intelligence Unit, Country Profile and Quarterly Economic Review.
> Frost & Sullivan, Political Risk Yearbook.

You may also be able to locate useful information through the World Wide Web.

Chapter 19

What Determines Exchange Rates in the Short Run?

Overview

This chapter examines short-run movements in exchange rates. It presents the version of the asset market approach to exchange rates that focuses on debt securities and the relationships between the current spot exchange rate, interest rates, and the expected future spot exchange rate. It makes heavy use of the concepts of international financial investment previously presented in Chapter 17. It also shows how "overshooting" of exchange rates in the short and medium runs eventually reverts to the long run in which purchasing power parity (PPP, as previously discussed in Chapter 18) holds.

The asset market approach presented in the text is based on the uncovered interest parity relationship, presuming that this relationship holds approximately if not exactly. The basic discussion examines the pressure on the current spot exchange rate if one of the other three rates changes, with the other two held constant. If the domestic interest rate increases, then the foreign currency depreciates (the home currency appreciates). If the foreign interest rate increases, then the foreign currency appreciates. (The text notes that what really matters is the change in the interest differential.)

If the expected future spot exchange rate value of the foreign currency increases, then the current spot exchange rate value of the foreign currency increases. Many different things can influence the expected future spot exchange rate. First, if expectations simply extrapolate recent trends, then a bandwagon is possible. Speculation then may be based on destabilizing expectations—expectations formed without regard to the economic fundamentals—and (speculative) bubbles can occur. Second, if expectations are based on a belief that exchange rates eventually follow PPP, then they lead to stabilizing speculation—speculation that tend to move the exchange rate toward a value consistent with the economic fundamentals of national price levels. Third, expectations are affected by various kinds of news about economic and political circumstances.

Both the domestic interest rate and the expected future exchange rate can change at the same time. If the increase in the nominal domestic interest rate is caused by a higher expected rate of inflation, then it may also be accompanied by an expectation (based on PPP) that the domestic currency will depreciate in the future. In this case, there is no simple prediction for the pressure on the current spot exchange rate. If instead the higher domestic interest rate is not accompanied by an expectation of higher future inflation, then there is no obvious reason to expect a depreciation of the country's currency. This increase in both the nominal and real interest rate results in pressure for the current spot exchange rate value of the country's currency to appreciate.

How do we get from the short run in which portfolio adjustments by international investors place the major pressures on exchange rates to the long run of PPP? We can view this as a process in which the exchange rate overshoots (relative to the value consistent with PPP) in the short run, and then (gradually) reverts to PPP in the long run. This can be seen most clearly by considering an abrupt change in the domestic money supply. The additional (and presumably realistic) assumption is that product price levels adjust slowly toward the level consistent with the quantity theory equation. If the domestic money supply increases abruptly, then, at first, the domestic price level does not rise much, but eventually it will. With the increase in the money supply (and not so much of an increase in money demand at first), domestic interest rates decrease. In addition, investors expect that eventually the foreign currency will appreciate (the domestic currency will depreciate) relative to its initial value, because the domestic price level eventually will be higher (PPP in the long run). For both of these reasons (lower interest rate and expected appreciation of the foreign currency relative to its initial value), investors shift their investments toward foreign-currency assets. This causes an abrupt, large appreciation of the foreign currency—more than is consistent with the small amount of change in the domestic price level in the short run, and also more than is consistent with the long run changes in the price level. Once the exchange rate value of the foreign currency overshoots in the short run, it then is expected to and does decline back toward the long run value that is consistent with PPP. In fact, this subsequent expected depreciation of the foreign currency is necessary to reestablish uncovered interest parity. The overall return on foreign-currency assets is then lowered by the expected depreciation of the foreign currency, so that it is about equal to the lower domestic return resulting from the lower domestic interest rate.

The chapter concludes with a discussion of how difficult it is to predict exchange rate movements in the short run. Generally, we cannot beat the naive model of a random walk, which predicts that the exchange rate in the future will simply be the same as the exchange rate today. A major reason for this inability to forecast is that the current spot exchange rate reacts quickly and strongly to unexpected (and therefore unpredictable) news. A second reason may be that traders and investors form their short-run expectations of exchange rates based not only on economic fundamentals but also on recent trends. The expectations are then self-confirming, resulting in bubbles in the movement of exchange rates over time.

Tips

This chapter presents basic concepts and tools that are useful in understanding short-run movements in exchange rates. One point is clear—short-run pressures on major currencies and many others result from portfolio adjustments or financial repositioning by international investors and traders. Beyond this, we must be somewhat humble. While we have some understanding of the basic reasons for these adjustments and repositioning, there is also much that we cannot explain or predict by relatively simple theories.

The presentation of the pressures on the current spot rate from changes in the other rates emphasizes two compatible explanations. The first is the flow pressure on the current spot rate that results from financial repositioning of international portfolios. This seems to be the best way to get students to grasp intuitively the logic of the relationships. The second is the rate adjustment necessary to reestablish (at least approximately) uncovered interest parity. This is consistent with a stock equilibrium in the holding of financial assets.

The more complicated version of the asset market approach that emphasizes variations in risk premiums is mentioned in footnote 2. We do not develop this version in the text—it seems needlessly complicated, and empirical tests generally fail to show that it is important.

Suggested answers to questions and problems
(in the textbook)

2. Disagree. The first part of the statement is true. Flows of foreign financial investment add to demand for the country's currency in the foreign exchange market, so the country's currency tends to appreciate. But the second part of the statement is not true. Outflows as foreign investors pull their investments out of the country add to the supply of the country's currency in the foreign exchange market, so the country's currency tends to depreciate.

4. The country's government should increase the country's interest rates in order to prevent the currency from depreciating. In making their decisions, foreign investors' expected return on investments in assets denominated in this country's currency is the interest rate earned on these assets minus the expected depreciation of the country's currency. Even if international financial investors continue to expect the currency to depreciate, the higher interest rate can be used to stem any capital outflow that could put immediate downward pressure on the exchange-rate value of the country's currency.

6. a. The euro is expected to appreciate at an annual rate of approximately $((1.206 - 1.200)/1.200) \cdot (360/180) \cdot 100 = 1\%$. The expected uncovered interest differential "in favor of Europe" is $5\% + 1\% - 6\% = 0$, so uncovered interest parity holds (approximately).
   b. If the interest rate on 180-day dollar-denominated bonds declines to 5%, then the spot exchange rate is likely to increase—the euro will appreciate, the dollar depreciate. At the initial current spot exchange rate, the initial expected future spot exchange rate, and the initial euro interest rate, the expected uncovered interest differential shifts in favor of investing in euro-denominated bonds (the expected uncovered differential is now positive, $5\% + 1\% - 5\% = 1\%$ "in favor of Europe"). The increased demand for euros in the spot exchange market tends to appreciate the euro. If the euro interest rate and the expected future spot exchange rate remain unchanged, then the current spot rate must change immediately to be $1.206/euro, to reestablish uncovered interest parity. When the current spot rate jumps to this value, the euro's exchange rate value is not expected to change in value subsequently during the next 180 days. The dollar has depreciated, and the uncovered differential again is zero ($5\% + 0\% - 5\% = 0$).

8. a. For uncovered interest parity to hold, investors must expect that the rate of change in the spot exchange-rate value of the yen equals the interest rate differential, which is zero. Investors must expect that the future spot value is the same as the current spot value, $0.01/yen.
   b. If investors expect that the exchange rate will be $0.0095/yen, then they expect the yen to depreciate from its initial spot value during the next 90 days. Given the other rates, investors tend to shift their investments toward dollar-denominated investments. The extra supply of yen (and demand for dollars) in the spot exchange market results in a

decrease in the current spot value of the yen (the dollar appreciates). The shift to expecting that the yen will depreciate (the dollar appreciate) sometime during the next 90 days tends to cause the yen to depreciate (the dollar to appreciate) immediately in the current spot market.

10. a. The tightening typically leads to an immediate increase in the country's interest rates. In addition, the tightening probably also results in investors' expecting that the exchange-rate value of the country's currency is likely to be higher in the future. The higher expected exchange-rate value for the currency is based on the expectation that the country's price level will be lower in the future, and PPP indicates that the currency will then be stronger. For both of these reasons, international investors will shift toward investing in this country's bonds. The increase in demand for the country's currency in the spot exchange market causes the current exchange-rate value of the currency to increase. The currency may appreciate a lot because the current exchange rate must "overshoot" its expected future spot value. Uncovered interest parity is reestablished with a higher interest rate and a subsequent expected depreciation of the currency.

   b. If everything else is rather steady, the exchange rate (the domestic currency price of foreign currency) is likely to decrease quickly by a large amount. After this jump, the exchange rate may then increase gradually toward its long-run value—the value consistent with PPP in the long run.

Chapter 20

Government Policies Toward the Foreign Exchange Market

Overview

The first half of this chapter examines types of government policies toward the foreign exchange market and provides analysis of government intervention and exchange controls. The second half examines the actual policies that governments have adopted during the past 130 years.

Government policies toward the foreign exchange market exist for a variety of reasons, including to reduce variability in exchange rates, to keep the exchange value of its currency either high or low, or to raise national pride in a steady or strong currency. The two major aspects of government policies toward the foreign exchange market are policies toward the exchange rate itself and policies that permit or restrict access to the foreign exchange market. Government-imposed restrictions on the use of the foreign exchange market are called exchange controls, which may be broad-based or may be applied only to some types of transactions (e.g., capital controls).

The basic choice that a government faces with its policy toward the exchange rate itself is between an exchange rate that is floating and one that is set or fixed by the government. In the polar case of a clean float the government permits private market demand and supply to set the exchange rate with no direct involvement by government officials. In a managed float or dirty float the government officials do intervene at times to try to influence the exchange rate, which otherwise is driven by private demand and supply.

If the government chooses to impose a fixed exchange rate, there are three additional choices that the government faces. First, what to fix to? Answers could include gold (or some other commodity), the U.S. dollar or some other single currency, or a basket of currencies. (With the exception of the specific examination of the gold standard, subsequent discussion assumes that a fix is to one or several foreign currencies.) Second, when to change the fixed exchange rate? Never is a polar case, but it probably is not completely credible (and we often then speak of a pegged exchange rate instead of a fixed exchange rate). If occasionally, we call the system an adjustable peg. If often, we have a crawling peg. The choice of when to change the peg is closely related to how wide is the band around the central or par value chosen for the fix. Third, how to defend the fixed rate? There are four basic ways—official intervention in which the government buys and sells currencies; exchange controls, in which the government tries to suppress excess demand or supply; altering domestic interest rates to influence short-term international capital flows; and adjusting the country's macroeconomic position to make it fit the fixed exchange rate. Of course, the government also has a fifth option—to alter the fixed rate or shift to a floating rate.

The first line of defense is often official intervention. If the country's currency is experiencing pressure toward depreciation, the country's monetary authority can defend the fixed rate (at least, at the edge of the band) by entering the foreign exchange market to buy domestic currency and sell foreign currency. The intervention is financing the country's official settlements balance deficit and preventing this excess private demand for foreign currency from driving the foreign currency's value above the top of the band. The monetary authority obtains the foreign currency that they sell into the market by using their holding of official reserves or by borrowing foreign currency. In addition, by buying domestic currency, the monetary authority is removing domestic money from the economy, which tends to lower the domestic money supply. (Chapter 22 takes up the implications of this induced change in the domestic money supply.) Analysis of defending against appreciation of the country's currency follows similar logic, with "the directions reversed."

If the imbalance in the country's official settlements balance is temporary, then official intervention that smoothes the time path of the exchange rate can enhance the country's economic well-being (although stabilizing private speculation could do the same thing without government intervention). If the disequilibrium is ongoing or fundamental rather than temporary, then intervention alone is not likely to be able to sustain the fixed exchange rate. Instead, the government must shift to one of the other defenses or devalue. A key problem here is that it is not easy for officials to judge whether a payments imbalance is temporary or fundamental.

Exchange controls are used by many countries, especially developing countries. They cause economic inefficiency analogous to quantitative limits (quotas) on imports. They also incur substantial administrative costs. Efforts to evade them lead to bribery and parallel markets.

The second half of the chapter surveys exchange rate regimes used during the past century. During the gold standard era (1870-1914), most countries pegged their currencies to gold, with each central bank willing to buy and sell gold in exchange for its own currency. This implies that the exchange rates between currencies are also fixed (within a band resulting from the transactions costs of moving gold). Britain was at the center of the system. The gold standard looked successful because it was not subject to severe shocks (until it was suspended during World War I) and because success was defined leniently, given that governments were not so concerned with stabilizing their macroeconomies.

The interwar period brought instability. In the years after the World War I Britain made the mistake of attempting to return to its prewar gold parity. Germany suffered from hyperinflation, and other European countries also experienced substantial inflation. The early 1930s brought panics that led to the general abandonment of the gold standard. Compared with the gold standard era, exchange rates were quite variable. Experts at the time concluded that this experience showed the instability of flexible exchange rates, so that the world should return to fixed exchange rates. More recent analysis of this period concludes almost the opposite—that it shows the futility of trying to keep exchange rates fixed in the face of severe shocks and unstable domestic monetary and fiscal policies.

A compromise between the United States and Britain led to an agreement in 1944 that established the Bretton Woods System, a regime of adjustable pegged exchange rates with the International Monetary Fund as a multilateral organization to oversee the system and provide additional reserves to finance temporary deficits. While this system looked successful for almost two decades, it also had two defects. One was that it set up one-way speculative gambles when currencies were in trouble The second concerned the role of the U.S. dollar in the system. As the system developed, other countries pegged their currencies to the dollar, and the U. S. government was committed to buy or sell gold for dollars with other central banks. Continuing U.S. payments deficits in the 1960s led some other countries to amass large holdings of U.S. dollar-denominated assets as official reserves. Confidence that the U.S. government could continue to honor the official gold price dwindled. The U.S. government was unwilling to contract the U.S. economy to reduce the U.S. payments deficits. Instead, the private market for gold was freed in 1968. U.S. payments deficits continued. In 1971 the U.S. government suspended convertibility of dollars into gold and imposed a temporary tariff on all imports until other countries agreed to revalue their currencies (so that the dollar would be devalued). The Smithsonian Agreement of December 1971 attempted to reestablish the system (with many other currencies being revalued), but the pegged rate system was abandoned by the major countries in 1973.

The current system is often described as a system of managed floating exchange rates, and the trend is generally in this direction. But there is also much official resistance to market-driven exchange rates. Some of the resistance is seen in the active management of floating exchange rates. More dramatically, the countries of the European Union have attempted to create a zone of stability in Europe, first by using the snake within the tunnel, then through the Exchange Rate Mechanism of the European Monetary System, and now with European Monetary Union and the euro. A goodly number of countries maintain fixed or heavily managed exchange rates. However, the series of exchange rate crises of the 1990s show how difficult it is for a government to defend a fixed or a heavily managed exchange rate in the face of wide swings in speculative international financial flows.

The actual current system is in many ways a nonsystem—countries can choose almost any exchange rate policies that they want, and there is much variety. Two major blocs of currencies exist—one is the U.S. dollar and the currencies fixed to it, and the other is the countries adopting the euro and other countries fixed to the euro. A number of countries have floating exchange rates for their currencies, with a greater or lesser degree of "management." Yet other countries use a fixed exchange rate to another currency, a fixed exchange rate to a basket of currencies, or a crawling pegged exchange rate.

Tips

This is a long chapter. For reading assignments it is possible to split the chapter into two or three assignments. The first would cover the concepts and analysis of government policies toward the foreign exchange market (through the section on "Exchange Control"). The second would cover the experience of the past century, and this could be either the rest of the chapter or all but the last section on the current system. If the latter is used, then a third assignment would cover the current system. The two-assignment approach presumably would be useful if all of this material is covered in class in the order that it is presented in the text. The three-assignment approach would be useful, for instance, if the material on the history of regimes is deferred until later in the course. In this latter approach, it still seems useful to describe the current system before the material of Part IV is covered in the course, but the sections on regime history would be shifted to later in the course.

Figure 20.9 is an excellent description of the current system. Although it is based on the table in the *International Financial Statistics*, we had to rework this information and add other information to create Figure 20.9. In 1999 the International Monetary Fund substantially altered the way that it reports information on countries' exchange rate policies in the *International Financial Statistics*, and as a class handout the new format unfortunately is probably less useful than the old format.

Suggested Answers to Questions and Problems

(in the textbook)

2. We often use the term pegged exchange rate to refer to a fixed exchange rate, because fixed rates generally are not fixed forever. An adjustable peg is an exchange rate policy in which the "fixed" exchange rate value of a currency can be changed from time to time, but usually it is changed rather seldom (for instance, not more than once every several years). A crawling peg is an exchange rate policy in which the "fixed" exchange rate value of a currency is changed often (for instance, weekly or monthly), sometimes according to indicators such as the difference in inflation rates.

4. Disagree. If a country is expected to impose exchange controls that will make it more difficult to move funds out of the country in the future, investors are likely to try to shift funds out of the country now before the controls are imposed. The increase in supply of domestic currency into the foreign exchange market (or increase in demand for foreign currency) puts downward pressure on the exchange rate value of the country's currency— the currency tends to depreciate.

6. a. The market is attempting to depreciate the pnut (appreciate the dollar) toward a value of 3.5 pnuts per dollar, which is outside of the top of the allowable band (3.06 pnuts per dollar). In order to defend the pegged exchange rate, the Pugelovian monetary authorities could use official intervention to buy pnuts (in exchange for dollars). Buying pnuts prevents the pnut's value from declining (selling dollars prevents the dollar's value from rising). The intervention satisfies the excess private demand for dollars at the current pegged exchange rate.

  b. In order to defend the pegged exchange rate, the Pugelovian government could impose exchange controls in which some private individuals who want to sell pnuts and buy dollars are told that they cannot legally do this (or cannot do this without government permission, and not all requests are approved by the government). By artificially restricting the supply of pnuts (and the demand for dollars), the Pugelovian government can force the remaining private supply and demand to "clear" within the allowable band. The exchange controls attempt to stifle the excess private demand for dollars at the current pegged exchange rate.

  c. In order to defend the pegged exchange rate, the Pugelovian government could increase domestic interest rates (perhaps by a lot). The higher domestic interest rates shift the incentives for international capital flows toward investments in Pugelovian bonds. The increased flow of international financial capital into Pugelovia increases the demand for pnuts on the foreign exchange market. (Also, the decreased flow of international financial capital out of Pugelovia reduces the supply of pnuts on the foreign exchange market.) By increasing the demand for pnuts (and decreasing the supply), the Pugelovian government can induce the private market to clear within the allowable band. The increased domestic interest rates attempt to shift the private supply and demand curves so that there is no excess private demand for dollars at the current pegged exchange rate value.

8. a. The gold standard was a fixed rate system. The government of each country participating in the system agreed to buy or sell gold in exchange for its own currency at a fixed price of gold (in terms of its own currency). Because each currency was fixed to gold, the exchange rates between currencies also tended to be fixed, because individuals could arbitrage between gold and currencies if the currency exchange rates deviated from those implied by the fixed gold prices.

   b. Britain was central to the system, because the British economy was the leader in industrialization and world trade, and because Britain was considered financially secure and prudent. Britain was able and willing to run payments deficits that permitted many other countries to run payments surpluses. The other countries used their surpluses to build up their holdings of gold reserves (and of international reserves in the form of sterling-denominated assets). These other countries were satisfied with the rate of growth of their holdings of liquid reserve assets, and most countries were able to avoid the crisis of running low on international reserves.

   c. During the height of the gold standard, from about 1870 to 1914, the economic shocks to the system were mild. A major shock—World War I—caused many countries to suspend the gold standard.

   d. Speculation was generally stabilizing, both for the exchange rates between the currencies of countries that were adhering to the gold standard, and for the exchange rates of countries that temporarily allowed their currencies to float.

10. a. The Bretton Woods system was an adjustable pegged exchange rate system. Countries committed to set and defend fixed exchange rates, financing temporary payments imbalances out of their official reserve holdings. If a "fundamental disequilibrium" in a country's international payments developed, the country could change the value of its fixed exchange rate to a new value.

    b. The United States was central to the system. As the Bretton Woods system evolved, it became essentially a gold-exchange standard. The monetary authorities of other countries committed to peg the exchange rate values of their currencies to the U.S. dollar. The U.S. monetary authority committed to buy and sell gold in exchange for dollars with other countries' monetary authorities at a fixed dollar price of gold.

    c. To a large extent speculation was stabilizing, both for the fixed rates followed by most countries, and for the exchange rate value of the Canadian dollar, which floated during 1950-62. However, the pegged exchange rate values of currencies sometimes did come under speculative pressure. International investors and speculators sometimes believed that they had a one-way speculative bet against currencies that were considered to be "in trouble." If the country did manage to defend the pegged exchange rate value of its currency, the investors betting against the currency would lose little. They stood to gain a lot of profit if the currency was devalued. Furthermore, the large speculative flows against the currency required large interventions to defend the currency's pegged value, so that the government was more likely to run so low on official reserves that it was forced to devalue.

12. a. A number of countries (37 countries at the beginning of 1999) peg their currencies to the U.S. dollar. A number of European countries have fixed their currencies to the new euro (and will replace their national currencies with the euro), and, in addition, a number of other countries peg their currencies to the euro.

b. The other major currencies that float independently include (as of the beginning of 1999) the Japanese yen, the British pound, the Canadian dollar, and the Swiss franc.

c. The exchange rates between the U.S. dollar and the other major currencies have been floating since the early 1970s. The movements in these rates exhibit trends in the long run—over the entire period since the early 1970s. The rates also show substantial variability or volatility in the short and medium runs—periods of less than one year to periods of several years. The long run trends appear to be reasonably consistent with the economic fundamentals emphasized by purchasing power parity—differences in national inflation rates. The variability or volatility in the short or medium run is controversial. It may simply represent rational responses to the continuing flow of economic and political news that has implications for exchange rate values. The effects on rates can be large and rapid, because overshooting occurs as rates respond to important news. However, some part of the large volatility may also reflect speculative bandwagons that lead to bubbles that subsequently burst.

Chapter 21

How Does the Open Macroeconomy Work?

Overview

This chapter provides a framework and model for analyzing international macroeconomics. We judge the performance of a national economy against two objectives. Internal balance involves both full employment and price stability or an acceptable rate of inflation. External balance involves a reasonable and sustainable makeup of the country's international payments, taken to be approximately an official settlements balance that is zero. The framework generally assumes that the domestic price level is sticky or sluggish in the short run, although it does respond to supply and demand conditions beyond the short run.

In the short run (and within the economy's supply capabilities), domestic production is determined by aggregate demand: $Y = AD = C + I_d + G + (X - M) = E + (X - M)$, where Y is both domestic production and national income, and E is national expenditure on goods and services. Consumption C is a positive function of Y (inclusive of the effects of taxes T), and real domestic investment I_d is a negative function of the interest rate i. Imports M are a positive function of Y, according to the marginal propensity to import m.

If the interest rate and price level are constant, then the equilibrium is the level of real GDP (and income) that equals desired aggregate demand at that level of income, or, equivalently, the level of real GDP for which desired national saving S equals desired domestic and foreign investment $I_d + I_f$, given that X - M is (approximately) equal to I_f. The spending multiplier shows how equilibrium GDP responds to changes in any component of aggregate demand. The spending multiplier in a small open economy is $1/(s + m)$, where s is the marginal propensity to save (including any "forced saving" causes by the tax system). The multiplier is smaller than in a comparable closed economy (in which m is zero). For a large country whose trade noticeably affects domestic production in other countries, foreign income repercussions increase the true spending multiplier. A change in this large country's income changes its imports, which changes foreign exports by enough to alter foreign production and income. The change in foreign income changes foreign imports, which changes the first country's exports, leading to a further change in this country's production and income.

The IS-LM-FE model provides a more complete framework for analyzing the open macroeconomy. It is intended to show the determination of the short-run equilibrium levels of the country's real GDP and interest rate while also indicating the state of the country's official settlements balance (or, equivalently, the pressure on the exchange rate value of the country's currency). We are relaxing the assumption that the interest rate is steady.

The downward-sloping IS curve shows all combinations of Y and i that represent equilibrium in the domestic product market. A change in an influence on aggregate demand other than Y or i results in a shift in the IS curve. The upward-sloping LM curve shows all combinations of Y and i that represent equilibrium in the money market. A change in the money supply or a change in an influence on money demand other than Y or i results in a shift in the LM curve. The intersection of the IS and LM curves shows the short-run equilibrium values for real GDP and the interest rate.

The FE curve shows all combinations of Y and i that result in a zero official settlements balance. If the country's current account balance CA is a negative function of Y (because of import demand), and the country's (nonofficial) capital account KA is a positive function of i (because of the incentive for international capital flows), the FE curve generally slopes upward. A point above or to the left of the FE curve indicates that the country's official settlements balance is in surplus; a point below or to the right indicates a payments deficit. Given the marginal propensity to import, how flat or steep the FE curve is depends on how responsive international capital flows are to interest rate changes. The more responsive, the flatter the FE curve. In the extreme, with perfect capital mobility the FE curve is a horizontal line. A change in an influence on the current or capital accounts other than Y or i causes a shift in the FE curve. The text also notes that the ability of a higher domestic interest rate to attract inflows of capital probably falls off beyond a short time period.

As the economy moves beyond the short run, the price level does change, for three basic reasons. First, most countries have some amount of ongoing inflation. Second, strong or weak aggregate demand (relative to the economy's supply capabilities) puts pressure on the price level—strong demand causes overheating and weak demand causes a "discipline" effect. Third, price shocks, including oil price shocks and large, abrupt changes in the exchange rate value of the country's currency, can change in the price level.

The final piece of the framework that we develop in the text is that the country's exports and imports depend on international price competitiveness, in addition to depending on national incomes. The price of foreign-produced traded products relative to the price of home-produced substitute products is $P_f \cdot r / P$. (In Part IV we drop the s subscript from the spot exchange rate r, to simplify the notation.) This ratio is the real exchange rate introduced in Chapter 18. The country's demand for imports is a negative function of this price ratio, while demand for the country's exports is positive function. A change in price competitiveness causes a change in net exports, so that both the IS and the FE curves shift.

Tips

We present a framework that can be used to analyze both fixed (Chapter 22) and floating (Chapter 23) exchange rates. Clearly, any one framework is not perfect, but we believe that this framework (the Mundell-Fleming model) is a good framework that includes a large number of relationships that must be juggled in analyzing the open macroeconomy.

We have chosen to focus more on the complete model, and to reduce the treatment of spending multipliers by presenting the explicit formula for only the small, open-economy multiplier. Foreign income repercussions are covered intuitively and with examples. An instructor who wants to cover more on multipliers may want to prepare a class handout of a few pages that works through multipliers with foreign income repercussions.

Suggested answers to questions and problems

(in the textbook)

2.   Disagree. The recession in the United States reduces U.S. national income, so U.S. residents reduce spending on all kinds of things, including spending on imports. The decrease in U.S. imports is a decrease in the exports of other countries, including Europe's exports to the United States. The reduction in European exports reduces production in Europe, so the growth of real GDP in Europe declines. A recession in the United States is likely to lower the growth of European real GDP.

4. a.   The spending multiplier in this small open economy is about 1.82 (= 1/(0.15 + 0.4)). If real spending initially declines by $2 billion, then domestic product and income will decline by about $3.64 billion (= 1.82 × $2 billion)

     b.   If domestic product and income decline by $3.64 billion, then the country's imports will decline by about $1.46 billion (= $3.64 billion × 0.4).

     c.   The decrease in this country's imports reduces other countries' exports, so foreign product and income decline.

     d.   The decline in foreign product and income reduce foreign imports, so the first country's exports decrease. This reinforces the change (decline) in the first country's domestic product and income—an example of foreign-income repercussions.

6.   External balance is the achievement of a reasonable and sustainable makeup of a country's overall balance of payments with the rest of the world. While specifying a precise goal is not simple, we often presume that achieving a balance of approximately zero in a country's official settlements balance is external balance. The FE curve shows all combinations of interest rate and domestic product that result in a zero balance for the country's official settlements balance. Thus, any point on the FE curve is consistent with this concept of external balance.

8. a.   A decrease in government spending tends to decrease domestic product (and decrease interest rates because the government has to borrow less when it has a smaller budget deficit). Thus, the IS curve shifts to the left (or down).

     b.   An increase in foreign demand for the country's exports increases the country's domestic product. Thus, the IS curve shifts to the right (or up).

     c.   An increase in the interest rate does not shift the IS curve. Rather, it results in a movement along the IS curve.

10. a.   Imports increase, according to the marginal propensity to import.

     b.   Our exports decrease, as foreign imports decrease according to the foreign marginal propensity to import.

c. This makes our products relatively more expensive, and foreign products relatively less expensive. The price ratio (or real exchange rate) $P_f \cdot r/P$ decreases if P increases. The reduction in the price competitiveness of our products internationally tends to decrease our exports and increase our imports.

d. This makes our products relatively less expensive, and foreign products relatively more expensive. The price ratio (or real exchange rate) $P_f \cdot r/P$ increases if P_f increases more than P. The increase in the price competitiveness of our products internationally tends to increase our exports and decrease our imports.

Chapter 22

Internal and External Balance with Fixed Exchange Rates

Overview

This chapter presents the analysis of the macroeconomy of a country that has a fixed exchange rate. As noted in the introduction, this analysis is important because some countries currently have fixed exchange rates or floating rates that are so heavily managed that they resemble fixed rates, and because there are ongoing discussions of proposals to return to a system of fixed rates among the world's major currencies. We focus on defense of the fixed exchange rate through official intervention in the foreign exchange market.

To see the effects of defense through intervention, it is useful to describe the balance sheet of the country's central bank. The central bank holds two types of assets relevant to our discussion—official international reserve assets (R) and domestic assets (D). Its two relevant liabilities are domestic currency and deposits that (regular) banks place with the central bank. These two liabilities are the country's monetary base. With fractional reserve banking by regular banks, the country's money supply can be a multiple of the size of its base of "high-powered money."

When the country has an official settlements balance surplus, and its central bank intervenes to prevent its currency from appreciating, the central bank must sell domestic currency and buy foreign currency. This increases the central bank's holdings of official reserves and increases its liabilities as the domestic currency is added to the economy. The domestic money supply increases, probably by a multiple of the size of the intervention. If the money supply expands, then in the short run interest rates decrease. The capital account tends to deteriorate, and the increase in real spending and income increases the demand for imports, so the current account also tends to decrease. The overall payments surplus decreases. This is pictured as a downward shift in the LM curve toward a triple intersection of the new LM curve and the initial IS and FE curves. (In addition, the price level is likely to increase, at least beyond the short run, so that the current account also deteriorates as the country loses some international price competitiveness.) Intervention to prevent a currency from depreciating (in the face of an overall payments deficit) causes the opposite changes.

Rather than allowing these automatic adjustments toward external balance, the monetary authority can resist by sterilization—taking an offsetting domestic action (like an open market operation) to reduce or eliminate the effect of the intervention on the domestic money supply. This is a wait-and-see strategy. There are limits to how long the country can continue to run an overall payments imbalance. A key implication of this discussion is that a fixed exchange rate greatly constrains a country's ability to pursue an independent monetary policy, because the monetary policy must be consistent with maintaining the fixed rate.

A change in fiscal policy has two opposing effects on the country's overall payments balance. For instance, a shift to expansionary fiscal policy tends to increase both interest rates and real GDP, so the capital account tends to improve while the current account tends to deteriorate. If the former predominates, then the country's overall payments tend to go into surplus. If not sterilized, the intervention to defend the fixed exchange rate expands the domestic money supply, further expanding demand, domestic product, and income. In this case fiscal policy gains effectiveness to change real GDP. If the latter effect is larger (as it may be after as short period of time), then the opposite occurs. Both cases are shown as a shift first in the IS curve, with the position of the new IS-LM intersection being above or below the FE curve, depending on how steep or flat the FE curve is. The intervention then shifts the LM curve to a new triple intersection.

In the extreme case of perfect capital mobility (with investors expecting the fixed rate to be maintained), monetary policy has no independent effectiveness even in the short run, while fiscal policy has a strong (full spending multiplier) effect on real GDP. The FE curve is a flat line, and the LM curve is effectively this same flat line.

We can examine how shocks affect the economy of a country with a fixed exchange rate. A domestic monetary shock has a limited effect. A change in fiscal policy is an example of a domestic spending shock. An international capital flow shock shifts the FE curve. The intervention to defend the fixed exchange rate results in effects on the domestic economy. International trade shocks tend to cause payments imbalances that require intervention that changes the domestic money supply in the way that magnifies the effect of the shock on real GDP.

Countries often face both external and internal imbalances. Two combinations (high unemployment-payments surplus and excessive inflation-payments deficit) can be addressed with a change in government policy (expansionary or contractionary) but the other two seem to pose dilemmas. A possible short-run solution is a monetary-fiscal policy mix that follows the assignment rule. The change in monetary policy should address the external imbalance and the change in fiscal policy should address the internal imbalance. In practice countries often find it difficult or impossible to apply the assignment rule.

In the face of a payments imbalance, a country's government that is not willing to adjust domestic policies and the domestic economy may conclude that surrendering—changing or abandoning the fixed exchange rate—is best. For instance, with an overall payments deficit the country could devalue its currency. The devaluation should improve international price competitiveness, so net exports increase. This tends to decrease the payments deficit, and also to increase demand and domestic product. We can picture this as a rightward shift of the FE and IS curves. A key challenge for the country is to prevent the devaluation and the subsequent increase in demand from causing so much inflation that it eliminates the gain in price competitiveness.

The effect of a large, abrupt change in the exchange rate on the value of the country's current account (or trade) balance is not so straightforward. The value of the country's current account, measured in foreign currency (fc), is $CA = P^{fc}_x \cdot X - P^{fc}_m \cdot M$. The effects of a devaluation of the country's currency are: (1) no change or decrease in the foreign currency price of its exports (P^{fc}_x), (2) no change or increase in the volume of exports (X), (3) no change or decrease in the foreign currency price of its imports (P^{fc}_m), and (4) no change or decrease in the volume of imports (M). The response of the trade balance could be unstable (that is, the value of the balance could decline rather that improve) if the decrease in the foreign currency price of exports is large relative to the other changes—an extreme example is perfectly inelastic demands for exports and imports. The response will generally be stable (the balance will improve), at least if we allow enough time, because sufficiently high elasticities result in large enough changes in the trade volumes—one extreme example is the small-country case in which foreign elasticities are infinite so that foreign currency prices are fixed. (Appendix G derives a general formula relating demand and supply elasticities to the change in the value of the current account. It also discusses specific cases and the Marshall-Lerner condition.)

We generally expect that the trade balance deteriorates at first, because the price change occurs quickly while trade quantities change more slowly. After a moderate time period, the volume effects become large enough that the balance improves. In this case the response of the current account balance to a devaluation of the country's currency traces out a pattern called the J curve.

Tips

The analysis of each policy change or economic shock is deliberately presented first using schematics and words, and only then using the IS-LM-FE graph. Our goal is to impart the process of thinking logically about international macroeconomics. We believe that the graph is a great tool for organizing thinking, but it is not a substitute for understanding the logic of the relationships. Indeed, some instructors may wish to make the IS-LM-FE graphs optional if these are inappropriate for the preparation of the students and the objectives of the class. We believe that it is possible to present this material using both class discussion and the text while indicating to students that the IS-LM-FE graphs are not required and will not be tested.

The box on "A Tale of Three Countries" provides an application of the fixed-rate analysis to the experiences during the early 1990s of Germany, France, and Britain in the Exchange Rate Mechanism of the European Monetary System. Germany, the lead country, focused its policies on domestic performance issues arising from German unification. France successfully defended the pegged rate of the franc to the mark, but at substantial costs in terms of domestic macroeconomic performance. Britain surrendered and the depreciation of the pound permitted the British economy to reduce its unemployment rate, even as the rate in France and Germany continued to rise.

Suggested answers to questions and problems

(in the textbook)

2.   The increase in government spending affects both the current account and the capital account of the country's balance of payments. The increase in government spending increases aggregate demand, production, and income. The increase in income and spending increases the country's imports, so the current account tends to deteriorate (to become a smaller positive value or a larger negative value). The increase in production, income, and spending increases the demand for money. If the country's central bank does not permit the money supply to expand, then interest rates increase. (Similarly, the increase in the government budget deficit requires the government to borrow more to

finance its deficit, increasing interest rates.) The increase in interest rates increases the inflows of financial capital into the country (and decreases outflows), so that the capital account improves.

We are not sure about the effect of the policy change on the country's official settlements balance. It depends on the sizes of the changes in the two accounts. If the capital account improvement is larger (as we often expect in the short run), then the official settlements balance goes into surplus. If the current account deterioration is larger (as we often expect in the long run), then the official settlements balance goes into deficit.

If the official settlements balance goes into surplus, then the central bank must defend the fixed exchange rate through intervention by buying foreign currency and selling domestic currency. As the central bank sells domestic currency, this expands the domestic money supply if the intervention is unsterilized. This reinforces the expansionary thrust of the increase in government spending.

If the official settlements balance goes into deficit, then the central bank must defend the fixed exchange rate through intervention by selling foreign currency and buying domestic currency. As the central bank buys domestic currency, this contracts the domestic money supply if the intervention is unsterilized. This tends to reduce the expansionary thrust of the increase in government spending.

4.   The assignment rule says that a country with a fixed exchange rate can pursue both external balance and internal balance by assigning fiscal policy the task of achieving internal balance and assigning monetary policy the task of achieving external balance. The possible advantages of the assignment rule include: (1) it provides clear guidance to both types of policy, so that they can address macroeconomic stabilization even in cases in which apparent policy dilemmas exist, and (2) it directs each type of policy to focus on the target that each tends to care more about. The possible disadvantages of the assignment rule include: (1) it depends on the effect of interest rates on international capital flows, so that it will not work if capital flows are not that responsive to interest rate changes, or it may not work beyond the short-run period in which capital flows stop responding or tend to reverse, (2) lags in policy responses could destabilize the economy rather than stabilize it, (3) it may not be politically possible in some countries to run monetary policy separately from fiscal policy, (4) it may not be politically possible in some countries to run fiscal policy to address economic objectives such as internal balance, and (5) the policy mix can result in high domestic interest rates that can reduce domestic real investment and slow the growth of the country's supply capabilities in the long run.

6. a.   Pugelovian holdings of official international reserves decrease by $10 billion, a decline in holdings of foreign-exchange assets (assuming that the Pugelovian central bank did not just borrow the dollars used in the intervention).
  b.   The Pugelovian central bank is also buying pnuts in the intervention, so the Pugelovian money supply declines. Because this is removing high-powered money from the Pugelovian banking system, the Pugelovian money supply decreases by more than the

size of the intervention, with the actual decrease depending on the size of the money multiplier.

c.   The Pugelovian money supply does not change (or does not decrease as much) if the Pugelovian central bank sterilizes. To sterilize the intervention, the Pugelovian central bank would buy Pugelovian government bonds. As the central bank pays for the bonds, it is adding high-powered Pugelovian money back into the banking system. If it adds back the amount that was removed by the intervention, then the overall amount of high-powered money in the economy is unchanged, and the regular money supply can also be unchanged.

8. a.   If the country's capital account is always zero, then the country's interest rates have no direct effect on the country's balance of payments. The FE curve is a vertical line. (The country's overall payments balance is the same as its current account balance. The current account balance is affected by the country's domestic product and income through the demand for imports, but it is essentially not affected directly by the country's interest rates.)

   b.   The increase in foreign demand for exports shifts the IS curve to the right to IS' in the accompanying graph. The shock increases demand for the country's products, so domestic product and income tend to rise. The increase in foreign demand for exports shifts the FE curve to the right also, to FE'. At the initial level of income and domestic product, the current account and the overall payments balance go into surplus. A zero balance can be reestablished on the new FE' curve by increasing imports through an increase in domestic product and income. The LM curve is not directly affected, if this shock does not directly change money supply or money demand.

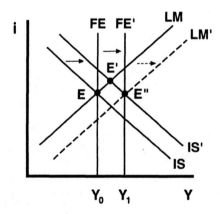

   c.   The rightward shift of the IS curve results in a new IS'-LM intersection at E' with some increase in the level of domestic product. The increase in domestic product and income also increases the country's imports. To proceed, let's examine the "normal" case in which the country then has a current account and overall payments surplus, because the increase in exports is larger than the initial increase in imports. This means that the intersection of the original LM curve and the new IS' curve is to the left of the new FE' curve. If the country's official settlements balance goes into surplus, then the country's central bank must intervene to defend the fixed exchange rate by buying foreign currency and selling domestic currency.

d. Assuming that the intervention is not sterilized, the intervention increases the country's money supply. The LM curve shifts to the right (or down). The country returns to external balance at the triple intersection E" when the LM curve has shifted to LM'. The country's domestic product and income have increased, from Y_0 to Y_1. If the country initially began with a high unemployment rate, then this is a movement toward internal balance. If the country initially began with internal balance or with an inflation rate that was considered too high, then this is a move away from internal balance, because the extra foreign and domestic spending on the country's products tends to drive the inflation rate up as the stronger demand exceeds the economy's supply capabilities.

10. a. The value of the Pugelovian current account, measured in foreign currency units, is:
$$CA = P^{fc}_x \cdot X - P^{fc}_m \cdot M.$$
If there is no change in quantities demanded (X and M are unchanged), then export and import markets must clear at the same supply prices. Pugelovian exporters receive the same competitive export price (measured in Pugelovian pnuts), so that the foreign-currency price of Pugelovian exports (P^{fc}_x) falls when the Pugelovian currency is devalued. Also, the foreign suppliers of Pugelovia's imports continue to charge the same foreign currency supply price (P^{fc}_m is unchanged). Thus, the Pugelovian current account deficit becomes larger, because the foreign-currency value of Pugelovian exports declines, and the foreign-currency value of Pugelovian imports is unchanged. Because the import demand elasticities are low (actually, zero), the response of the current account balance to the devaluation is perverse (it deteriorates rather than improves).

b. If Pugelovian firms keep their pnut prices the same, then the devaluation results in a decrease in the foreign-currency price of Pugelovian exports (P^{fc}_x). Generally, foreign buyers will buy a larger quantity of Pugelovian exports (X increases). If foreign firms keep the foreign-currency prices of their exports (P^{fc}_m) the same, then the devaluation results in a higher pnut price of imports in Pugelovia. Generally, Pugelovian buyers will buy a smaller quantity of imports (M falls). In this case, the Pugelovian current account could deteriorate, stay the same, or improve. Given the price changes (especially the decrease in the foreign-currency price of Pugelovian exports), the change in the value of the Pugelovian current account depends on the size of the responses in quantities demanded. If the responses are large enough (X rises and M falls enough), then the value of the Pugelovian current account deficit will decrease (its current account will improve). If the responses are small (X increases and M decreases only a little), then the value of the deficit will increase (the current account will deteriorate). The quantity changes are larger if the price elasticities of import demand in the two countries are larger (in absolute value).

Chapter 23

Floating Exchange Rates and Internal Balance

Overview

This chapter presents the analysis of the macroeconomy of a country that has a floating exchange rate. If government officials allow the exchange rate to float cleanly, then the exchange rate changes to achieve external balance.

With floating exchange rates monetary policy exerts strong influence on domestic product and income. A change in monetary policy results in a change in the country's interest rates. Both the current account and the capital account tend to change in the same direction. To keep the overall payments in balance, the exchange rate must change. The exchange rate change results in a change in international price competitiveness, assuming that it is larger or faster than any change in the country's price level—overshooting. The change in price competitiveness results in a change in net exports that reinforces the thrust of the change in monetary policy. We can picture the change in monetary policy as a shift in the LM curve, and then a shift in the IS and FE curves to a new triple intersection as the exchange rate and price competitiveness change.

With floating exchange rates the effect of a change in fiscal policy depends on how responsive international capital flows are to changes in interest rates. If capital flows are sufficiently responsive, then the exchange rate changes in the direction that counters the thrust of the fiscal policy change—an effect sometimes called international crowding out. If capital flows are not that responsive (or as we enter into the longer time period when the capital flows have slowed), the change in the current account dominates, so that the exchange rate changes in the direction that reinforces the thrust of the fiscal policy change. Both cases are shown as a shift in the IS curve, with the position of the intersection between the new IS curve and the LM curve being above or below the initial FE curve, depending on how flat or steep the FE curve is. The exchange rate change then shifts both the IS and FE curves toward a new triple intersection.

Domestic monetary shocks have strong effects on domestic product, with the exchange rate change reinforcing the thrust of the shock. The effects of domestic spending shocks depend on how responsive international capital flows are to changes in interest rates. International capital flow shocks affect the domestic economy by changing the exchange rate and the country's international price competitiveness. International trade shocks result in changes in the exchange rate that mute the effects of the shocks on domestic product.

While a cleanly floating exchange rate assures external balance, it does not assure internal balance, and changes in the floating exchange rate to achieve external balance can exacerbate an internal imbalance. Government monetary or fiscal policies may be used to address internal imbalances.

Changes in government policies adopted by one country can have spillover effects on other countries. International macroeconomic policy coordination involves some degree of joint determination of several countries' macroeconomic policies to improve joint performance. Efforts at policy coordination in the late 1970s and 1980s include the agreement at the Bonn Summit of 1978, the Plaza Agreement of 1985, and the Louvre Accord of 1987, but major efforts at coordination are infrequent. Countries disagree about goals and about how the macroeconomy works, and the benefits of coordination often are probably rather small.

The box on "Can Governments Manage the Float?" discusses whether selective intervention which is often sterilized can have significant effects on floating exchange rates between the major currencies. The conventional wisdom in the early 1980s was that sterilized intervention was ineffective. By the early 1990s several studies concluded that interventions were often successful in having a noticeable impact on the time path of the exchange rate. Intervention to manage floating exchange rates appears to be effective some but not all of the time.

Tips

This chapter is deliberately organized to parallel that of the previous Chapter 22 to the extent possible. This allows for carryover of students' insights and capabilities through Chapters 21, 22, and 23. It also results in clear contrasts between the behavior of a macroeconomy that has a fixed exchange rate and one that has a floating exchange rate. The contrasts in the effects of shocks are summarized in Figure 23.7, and other contrasts are reviewed in the next Chapter 24.

The method of analysis of policy changes and shocks used in the text is a bit mechanical, but it does seem to assist students in grasping the implications of floating exchange rates. We deliberately follow the same sequence for each change or shock: (1) the effects of the shock on the economy if (hypothetically) the exchange rate were unchanged, (2) the resulting pressure that causes a change in the floating exchange rate, and (3) the (additional) effects on the economy of this exchange rate change.

In presenting this material one should probably offer cautions that the effects do not always play out as suggested by the theory, because floating exchange rates do not always move in the directions indicated. This may be due to changes in investors' expectations of future exchange rates that are not captured by the approach, or it may be due to other shocks and news that are also influencing exchange rates.

The box on "U.S. Deficits: Twins or Cousins?" provides an application of the floating-rate analysis to the macroeconomic experience of the United States since 1980. The box shows how changes in the government budget deficit, the trade deficit, and the real exchange rate (with the expected lag) were closely correlated into the late 1980s—the two deficits were twins. However, for the United States during the 1990s, the two deficits were barely related, because the paths of private domestic saving and domestic real investment diverged.

Suggested answers to questions and problems

(in the textbook)

2.   The increase in government spending affects both the current account and the capital account of the country's balance of payments. The increase in government spending increases aggregate demand, production, and income. The increase in income and spending increases the country's imports, so the current account tends to deteriorate (become a smaller positive value or a larger negative value). The increase in production, income, and spending also increases the demand for money. If the country's central bank does not permit the money supply to expand, then interest rates increase. (Similarly, the increase in the government budget deficit requires the government to borrow more to finance its deficit, increasing interest rates.) The increase in interest rates increases the inflows of financial capital into the country (and decreases outflows), so that the capital account tends to improve.

The effect of this policy change on the exchange rate value of the country's currency depends on the effect on the official settlements balance. However, we are not sure about the effect of the policy change on the country's official settlements balance. It depends on the sizes of the changes in the two accounts. If the capital account improvement is larger (as we often expect in the short run), then the official settlements balance tends to go into surplus. If the current account deterioration is larger (as we often expect in the long run), then the official settlements balance tends to go into deficit.

If the official settlements balance tends to go into surplus, then the exchange rate value of the country's currency appreciates. The country loses international price competitiveness, and net exports tend to decrease. This reduces the expansionary thrust of the increase in government spending.

If the official settlements balance tends to go into deficit, then the exchange rate value of the country's currency depreciates. The country gains international price competitiveness, and net exports tend to increase. This reinforces the expansionary thrust of the increase in government spending.

4.   The decrease in demand for money tends to reduce domestic interest rates. The lower domestic interest rates encourage borrowing and spending, so domestic product and income increase because of the increase in domestic expenditure. The country's current account tends to deteriorate because the increase in domestic product and income increases imports. In addition, the country's capital account tends to deteriorate, because the lower domestic interest rates encourage a capital outflow. As the country's official settlements balance tends to go into deficit, the exchange rate value of the country's currency depreciates. The country gains international price competitiveness, and net exports tend to increase. This reinforces the expansion of domestic product and income.

Under fixed exchange rates, the central bank instead must resist the downward pressure on the exchange rate value of the country's currency by intervening in the foreign exchange market—the central bank must buy domestic currency and sell foreign currency. In buying domestic currency, the central bank reduces the domestic money supply (assuming that it does not sterilize). The contraction of the domestic money supply tends to counter the initial expansion of domestic product and income.

6. a. The contractionary monetary policy increases domestic interest rates, so borrowing and spending decrease. Domestic product and income tend to decline. The decline in demand puts downward pressure on the British inflation rate.

b. The increase in British interest rates draws a capital inflow, so Britain's capital account tends to improve. The decrease in British product and income reduces imports, so Britain's current account tends to improve. Thus, Britain's overall payments tend to go into surplus, so the exchange rate value of the pound tends to increase (the pound tends to appreciate).

c. As the pound appreciates, Britain tends to lose international price competitiveness (assuming overshooting—the currency appreciation occurs more quickly than the decline in the British inflation rate). British net exports tend to decline. This reinforces the contractionary thrust of British monetary policy on domestic product and income. In addition, it also reinforces the downward pressure on the British inflation rate, both because demand declines further, and because the appreciation tends to reduce the British pound prices of imports into Britain.

8. The increase in the foreign money supplies tends to lower foreign interest rates. The lower foreign interest rates spur borrowing and spending in foreign countries. The increase in foreign product and income increases the demand for imports, so our exports increase. In addition, the exchange rate values of foreign currencies decline, so that our currency appreciates. Foreign currencies depreciate because the overall foreign payments tend to go into deficit. The foreign current accounts tend to decline as foreign imports increase, and the foreign capital accounts tend to decline as the lower foreign interest rates spur capital outflows. The appreciation of our currency lowers our international price competitiveness, so our net exports tend to decrease. This counters the more direct effect of changes in international trade on our domestic product and income. This is an example of how floating exchange rates tend to reduce the domestic impact of an international shock, in this case a foreign monetary shock.

10. a. The increase in foreign demand for exports shifts the IS curve to the right to IS' in the accompanying graph. The shock increases demand for the country's products, so domestic product and income tend to rise. The increase in foreign demand for exports shifts the FE curve to the right also, to FE'. At the initial level of income and domestic product, the current account and the overall payments balance go into surplus. A zero balance can be reestablished on the new FE' curve by increasing imports through an increase in domestic product and income. The LM curve is not directly affected, if this shock does not directly change money supply or money demand.

b. The rightward shift of the IS curve results in a new IS'-LM intersection at E' with some increase in the level of domestic product. The increase in domestic product and income also increases the country's imports. To proceed, let's examine the "normal" case in which the country then tends to have a current account and overall payments surplus, because the increase in exports is larger than the initial increase in imports. This means that the intersection of the original LM curve and the new IS' curve is to the left of the new FE' curve. If the country's official settlements balance tends to go into surplus, then the exchange rate value of country's currency appreciates.

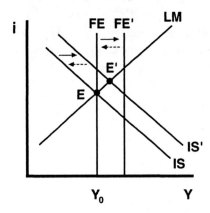

c. The currency appreciation reduces the country's international price competitiveness, and the country's net exports decrease. As the reduction in net exports reduces demand for the country's domestic product, the IS' curve shifts back toward the original IS curve. As the current account declines with the loss of price competitiveness, the FE' curve shifts back toward the original FE curve. If nothing else fundamental changes, then the curves shift back to their original positions, and the new triple intersection is back to the original one at E. There may be little or no effect on internal balance of all of this taken together (the international trade shock in favor of the country's exports plus the appreciation of the country's currency).

Chapter 24

National and Global Choices
Floating Rates and the Alternatives

Overview

This chapter provides a capstone to the discussion of international finance and international macroeconomics by examining the choice between fixed and floating exchange rates. Much of the discussion examines this choice from the point of view of a single country, but the discussion also examines some issues related to the functioning of the entire system.

The text examines five key issues that can influence a country's choice. Figure 24.2 presents a summary of implications of the key issues for the advantages of each policy choice.

First, different types of shocks have different effects, depending on which exchange rate policy is chosen. Internal shocks, especially domestic monetary shocks, are less disruptive to the domestic economy with a fixed exchange rate. External shocks, especially international trade shocks, are less disruptive with a floating exchange rate. If a country believes that it is mainly hit with internal shocks, it would favor a fixed rate; if it believed that it was mainly hit by external shocks, it would favor a floating rate.

Second, monetary policy is less effective as an independent policy influence on the domestic economy with a fixed exchange rate (compared to its effectiveness with a floating rate). Differences in the effectiveness of fiscal policy depend on the responsiveness of capital flows to interest rate changes. The key conclusion is that a country that desires to use monetary policy to address domestic objectives will favor a floating exchange rate.

Third, countries that have their currencies linked through fixed exchange rates must achieve consistency in their macroeconomic policies, so that the fixed rate can be defended and maintained. If countries have different goals, priorities, and policies, then they will favor floating exchange rates.

Fourth, the choice of exchange rate policy is linked to inflation rates in several ways. Countries that have fixed exchange rates between their currencies are committed to having similar inflation rates in the long run (an important specific example of the third point). Proponents of fixed rates argue that this imposes a discipline effect on countries that otherwise would tend to have high inflation rates. If the price discipline is stronger on countries that would tend to inflate and run payments deficits, then the overall average global inflation rate is likely to be lower with fixed rates. On the other hand, countries that might prefer to have even lower inflation rates (than the lead country in the fixed rate system) are likely to "import inflation" as their inflation rate tends to rise toward that of the lead country. Floating rates simply allow countries to have different inflation rates. In the 1970s it seemed that the average global inflation rate was higher with floating exchange rates, but the experience since the early 1980s indicates that the tendency toward higher inflation with floating rates is not that serious. What really matters is the resolve of the national monetary authorities.

Fifth, floating rates have been highly variable. The variability can increase exchange rate risk, which can discourage international transactions, especially trade in goods and services. In addition, overshooting can create signals for resource reallocations that are too strong. The defenders of floating rates indicate that this is a market doing what it is supposed to do—setting a market clearing price given demand and supply conditions at each time. The opponents of floating exchange rates believe that the variability is excessive, at least from the point of view of its effects on the macroeconomy.

Each country must make its own decision about its exchange rate policy. Several of these key issues seem to be important for most countries. Strong arguments in favor of a country's choosing a floating exchange rate are the use of changes in the floating exchange rate to achieve external balance, so that monetary policy can be used to pursue domestic objectives, the ability to set its own goals and policies, and the reduced need to hold official international reserves to defend against speculative attacks on the fixed rate. The strong argument in favor of a fixed rate is that floating rates are disturbingly variable. Many countries have shifted to a floating exchange rate during the past several decades. Even for countries that float, the government authorities typically use some form of management of the float. A managed floating exchange rate seems to be a reasonable compromise choice for many countries.

A number of countries maintain fixed exchange rates, but a fixed rate that is adjustable sometimes seems to invite speculative attack. In response, some countries are adopting exchange rate arrangements in which the fixed exchange rate value is very difficult to change. A currency board, such as that adopted by Argentina, Hong Kong, and several other countries, requires the country's monetary authority to focus almost completely on defending the fixed exchange rate through intervention, with almost no possibility for sterilizing the effects of any intervention. With "dollarization," used by Panama and few other very small countries, the country's government abolishes its own currency and uses the currency of some other country (e.g., the U.S. dollar).

The members of the European Union (EU) are pursuing an international fix—a monetary union in which exchange rates are permanently fixed among the currencies of the countries in the union and a single monetary authority conducts a unionwide monetary policy. As noted previously in Chapter 20, in 1979 the EU countries established the European Monetary System, and most became members of its Exchange Rate Mechanism (ERM), an adjustable pegged rate system among its members' currencies. By mid-1992 all EU members except Greece were members of the ERM, and most maintained their currencies within a band of plus or minus 2.25 percent around the central rates. Then a series of speculative attacks weakened the ERM—Britain and Italy left it in 1992, the bands for nearly all currencies were widened to plus or minus 15 percent in 1993, and several realignments were necessary for the central rates of the currencies of some other countries. After 1993 the exchange rates within the ERM were generally steady, and a number of countries joined or re-joined the ERM. The ERM experience provides examples of several points from earlier in the chapter. The ERM exchange rates generally were steadier than floating rates, and inflation rates in other ERM members decreased to the low levels of Germany.

But differences in priorities and policies led to the strains that weakened the system in the early 1990s.

At the same time as the turmoil in the ERM, the EU countries drafted and approved the Maastricht Treaty, which called for creation of European Monetary Union in 1999, for countries that met five criteria contained in the treaty. In 1998 eleven countries were deemed to meet the criteria and chose to join. On January 1, 1999, the union began, with the euro as a new common currency and the European Central Bank (ECB) conducting monetary policy for the union. Key gains from European Monetary Union are the elimination of exchange rate risk and eventually the elimination of the transaction costs of exchanging currencies. Key risks include questions about how effective the ECB will be in its conduct of monetary policy and the loss of national use of exchange rate changes and monetary policy to address shortcomings in national economic performance. Fiscal policy remains available, but may be constrained both by national politics and by limits imposed by the EU. Labor mobility between countries is low. While there are these risks, the member countries seem to be strongly committed politically to the monetary union.

Tips

One classroom exercise that can be both fun and challenging is to divide the class into several groups and have a class debate about the desirability of different exchange rate systems for NAFTA. For instance, one group could be the proponent of a rapid shift to monetary union, a second the proponent of fixed but adjustable exchange rates among the Canadian dollar, the U.S. dollar and the Mexican peso (a system like the European Exchange Rate Mechanism), and the third the proponent of continuing the floating exchange rates among the NAFTA currencies. If this is done without formal group preparation, then the instructor can call on a person from each group to present one point, and then rotate around the groups until most points have been made. Or, groups can meet and prepare formal statements of key arguments, with class presentations of the groups' statements. After any follow-on discussion, the class could end with a vote—if you were a Canadian (or a Mexican, or an American) politician or businessperson, what system would you favor?

Suggested answers to questions and problems

(in the textbook)

2. Probably agree, but with a caution. It is usually argued that the average rate of global inflation would tend to be lower if most countries adhered to a system of fixed exchange rates. Countries that succeed in maintaining fixed exchange rates among their currencies must have similar inflation rates in the long run. This tends to discipline countries that otherwise would drift or surge toward higher inflation rates. Furthermore, there is more pressure on countries with payments deficits to adjust than there is on surplus countries. In defending the fixed exchange rates, countries with payments deficits must intervene to buy their own currency. This tends to contract their money supplies and reduce their inflation rates. Thus, overall, the world tends toward less money growth and a lower average rate of world inflation. There is one caution, however. If the system has a lead country, then the inflation rate that forms the standard for the system is this country's

inflation rate. Some countries that otherwise would prefer to have an even lower inflation rate will find that their inflation rate is drifting up toward the rate in the lead country.

4.   Agree or disagree. If you say agree, then you will emphasize points like the following. With a clean floating exchange rate, the rate is set by private competitive supply and demand in the market. This rate is a market price that represents all information about currency values that is available at that time. Governments have no special information, so that they cannot improve on the clean float. Intervention by the government in the exchange market often seems to have little effect on exchange rate values. When it does have an impact, it distorts the exchange rate, usually for political purposes, especially to respond to the desires of powerful special interests.

If you disagree, then you will emphasize points like the following. Cleanly floating exchange rates are excessively variable, perhaps because private supply and demand are sometimes driven not by rational examination of information on the economic fundamentals, but rather by bandwagons and similar speculative behavior, or simply because exchange rates tend to overshoot their long-run values. Thus, a managed float permits a country to obtain many of the benefits of a floating exchange rate, including some policy independence and the ability to use exchange rate changes in the process of adjustment to external imbalances, while using intervention to limit wide swings and excessive variability in exchange rate values.

6. a.   These economists believe that the variability exists for good reasons, and that many of the supposed bad effects of exchange rate variability are not that large. They believe that the variability results from rational and reasonable responses of market participants, especially international investors, to various kinds of shocks and news. As economic and political conditions change, exchange rates should change to reflect the new information about the relative values of currencies. They believe that variability does not lead to risk that unreasonably reduces international transactions. Those engaged in international transactions like trade in goods and services have a variety of ways to hedge their exposures to exchange rate risk, including forward foreign exchange contracts as well as currency futures, options, and swaps.

    b.   These economists believe that the variability is excessive, and that the risks do have an undesirable impact on international transactions. They believe that the variability sometimes results from bandwagons and similar expectations that carry exchange rates away from their appropriate economic values. In addition, overshooting can cause exchange rates to deviate from their longer run values, even if the rates follow a path that is economically rational. They believe that some of the resulting exchange rate risk does have an impact on international transactions, because it is not possible to hedge perfectly and costlessly. Risk may especially affect real investments that support exports and similar international transactions, because the risk that must be hedged is further in the future, and because the payments at risk are themselves often of uncertain sizes. Furthermore, they believe that excessive rate movements that persist beyond the short run, such as the overshooting that can keep exchange rates away from their longer run values for a number of years, create signals for resource reallocations that are too large or too rapid.

8. The five convergence criteria are: (1) the country's inflation rate must be no more than 1.5 percentage points above the average inflation rate of the three lowest inflation EU countries, (2) the country's exchange rates must have been maintained within the ERM band with no realignments during the previous two years, (3) the country's long-term interest rate on government bonds must be no more than 2 percentage points above the average of the rates in the three lowest inflation countries, (4) the country's government budget deficit must be less than or equal to 3 percent of the value of its GDP, and (5) the country's gross government debt must be less than or equal to 60 percent of the value of its GDP. For the latter two criteria the country need not meet them exactly, as long as the country shows adequate progress toward achieving them in the near future.

    We can guess about the logic for each requirement. The inflation criterion shows that the country is ready to switch smoothly to fixed exchange rates with other low inflation countries. It is based on the logic of purchasing power parity—that countries must maintain similar inflation rates if fixed rates are to be sustained. The exchange rate criterion shows that the country already has been able to maintain a pegged exchange rate, so that it is ready to switch smoothly to completely fixed exchange rates. In addition, the criterion may be intended to limit a country's ability to use "one last" devaluation to gain a competitive edge in pricing just before it enters into "permanently" fixed exchange rates. The interest rate criterion may show that credit markets judge the country to be a good inflation rate risk and good credit risk. A country that is not expected to maintain a low inflation rate probably has to pay a higher interest rate on its long term debt. Its tendency toward higher inflation in the future would threaten the viability of the fixed exchange rates. Even worse, a country whose government might run into problems in repaying its debts also probably has to pay a higher interest rate on its long term government debt. If the government does then run into problems, the other countries may be forced to bail it out in order to defend the fixed exchange rates. The two criteria related to the government budget deficit and debt seem to be related to achieving fiscal policies that are not too different between the countries that enter into the fixed exchange rates. This may limit strains within the system. Especially, it keeps out countries who might favor more inflationary monetary policies to bail them out in the face of excessive government budget deficits and debt.

    Given the importance of having and maintaining similar inflation rates for the success of fixed exchange rates, the most important criterion is probably that related to the country's inflation rate. The criteria related to government budget deficits and debt seem to be the least important. A country that shifts to completely fixed exchange rates has given up the ability to use national monetary policy and exchange rate changes in seeking to address imbalances. This country may need to use fiscal policy more actively, including sometimes running large budget deficits. If the criteria also restrain the independence of fiscal policy, the country's government is left with little in the way of policy tools to address national imbalance.

10. Here are several arguments in favor of a Britain staying out of the European Monetary Union and instead maintaining its policy of an independently floating exchange rate for

the pound. First, changes in the floating exchange-rate value of the pound can be used in adjusting to reduce external imbalances that Britain might face. Changes in the exchange-rate value of the pound can also reduce the Britain's vulnerability to external shocks, including shocks coming from other EU countries. Second, adoption of floating exchange rates allows Britain to pursue its own monetary policy. Monetary policy can be used to seek internal balance, and Britain's government has a greater ability to pursue its own goals and priorities. The ability to use monetary policy to fight a British recession and high British unemployment can be especially valuable if fiscal policy is not flexible enough to be useful in pursuing internal balance, and if movements of labor between countries of the union are not likely to be large enough (or perhaps even not desirable) as a way to smooth cyclical differences between these countries. Third, those affected by the variability of floating exchange rates have a variety of means of hedging their exposures to exchange rate risks, including forward foreign exchange contracts and currency futures, options, and swaps. These contracts are available with very low transactions costs. Finally, the British inflation rate is best controlled by a British central bank that is committed to this goal. Although the European Central Bank is structured like the German central bank, it is also subject to political pressures that could reduce its commitment to maintaining low inflation, so there is no guarantee that Britain will have lower inflation if it joins the monetary union.

Chapter 25

The International Movement of Labor

Overview

This chapter examines the economics of labor migration, including the benefits and the costs to the migrants, the effects of migration on other groups and on the sending and receiving countries overall, the fiscal effects of migration, and government policies toward migration. It begins by examining the history of migration, focusing on immigration into the United States, Canada, and the European Union. For the United States and Canada, immigration was relatively large until the 1920s, was low in the 1930s, and has been higher since the 1950s. For the shorter history of the European Union, immigration was curtailed in the mid-1970s, but has increased again since the late 1980s.

We then examine the basic theory of migration, by picturing labor markets in the "North" and the "South" of the world. Higher wage rates in the North provide the incentive for migration, but migration is also limited by the economic and psychic costs of migration. The analysis shows that migrants themselves gain, workers remaining in the South gain, employers in the South lose, workers in the North lose, and employers in the North gain. The South overall (excluding the migrants who have left) loses, the North overall (again excluding the migrants) gains, and the world gains from this migration.

Migration can also cause what appear to be average-income paradoxes if the migrants are counted as part of the sending country before they migrate and part of the receiving country after they migrate. For instance, if migrants have below-average incomes in the sending country before they migrate, and below-average incomes in the receiving country after they migrate, the average income in the sending country rises with the emigration, but total income declines, and average income in the receiving country falls with the immigration, but total income rises. The paradox disappears if the migrants and their incomes are counted as being part of one or the other country both before and after they migrate.

The fiscal effects of migration have become increasingly controversial. In response to concerns about rising fiscal costs, laws in the United States have limited access of immigrants to some government programs. The fiscal effects are somewhat complicated. Migrants shift from paying taxes in the sending country to paying taxes in the receiving country. They also shift from public goods, transfer programs, and other goods and services provided by the sending country government to those provided by the receiving country government.

For the sending country the loss of tax payments is likely to loom the largest, especially for those who migrate in early adulthood. The loss is likely to be the largest for the "brain drain"—the migration of educated individuals who have often received schooling at the public expense and who would pay substantial taxes on their relatively high earnings. The sending country could attempt to address this net public-finance loss by imposing a tax on emigrants, or by encouraging the return of previous emigrants.

For a receiving country like the United States, the fiscal effects of immigration depend on whether providing government goods and services to the immigrants requires an expansion in spending on these goods and services, in order to maintain the same level of consumption value to natives in the country. Presumably, any transfer payments received by immigrants are an expansion of government expenditures, but the effects on other government goods and services are debatable. One way to examine this is to look at a snapshot for a single year. If all other government products are pure public goods, then for the United States in 1990 (and presumably other years as well) immigrants pay more in taxes than they expand government expenditures (in this case, just the transfer payments they receive)—the net fiscal effect would be positive. If immigrants take away natives' benefits for all other government goods and services (so that maintaining the same level of consumption value to natives would require an expansion of government spending), then for the United States in 1990 the net fiscal effect would be negative—the taxes paid by immigrants do not cover the extra government expenditures (in this case, both the transfer payments to the immigrants and the extra government spending needed for other government goods and services). The truth lies somewhere in between, so the issue remains controversial, and the balance seems to have shifted over time—in earlier years the case that immigrants were a net fiscal gain was stronger.

Another way to look at this is to examine the net effects over the entire lifetimes of immigrants and their descendants. One careful recent study of the United States concludes that the average net fiscal effect is slightly negative for the typical immigrant and substantially positive for the immigrant's descendants. In addition, the study concludes that the net fiscal effect of the immigrant depends on the immigrant's level of education, used as indicator of labor skill and earnings potential. Immigrants with a high school education or less impose a net cost; immigrants with some college provide a net benefit. Because the average education and earnings of immigrants has been declining relative to those of natives, for the United States since about 1980, the fiscal balance is probably shifting toward immigrants being a fiscal burden.

We should recognize several other possible effects of immigration that go beyond the labor-market and fiscal analyses. First, immigrants often bring external benefits through knowledge spillovers. Second, immigrants can bring external costs through increased congestion and crowding. Third, immigrants can raise social frictions based on bigotry, which can become severe during periods when the rate of immigration is high.

Our analysis has implications for the policies used by countries to limit immigration. First, the types of immigrant admitted have an impact on which native group suffers loss. Second, the types of immigrants admitted have an impact on the net fiscal effects. To gain greater fiscal benefits (and to minimize the negative impact on low-skilled native workers who already have low earnings), the receiving country should skew its immigration policies to favor young adults with some college education. However, for countries like the United States, this would mean shifting away from other worthy goals pursued by their current immigration policies, including family reunification and assisting refugees.

Tips

This topic is a sensitive one, and any presentation needs to keep its scientific standards up, by distinguishing what is known or plausibly estimated from what is common folklore.

The public-finance effects are an important issue. The chapter makes extensive use of George Borjas's recent estimates of possible fiscal effects of immigration into the United States. While these estimates are difficult, both for Borjas to derive and for you to present, students can master them. One helpful tip might be to focus on just one tax rate, say the 30% rate, in presenting the material in Figures 25.6 and 25.7.

This chapter can be assigned and covered in a course in conjunction with the material in Parts I and II. In fact, if only the "pure theory" material (the first two or three major sections of the chapter, before the material on public finance) is covered, this could be assigned right after Chapter 6.

Suggested answers to questions and problems

(in the textbook)

2.   First, in 1924, the United States passed a law that severely restricted immigration, using a system of quotas by national origin. Second, the Depression, with its very high rates of labor unemployment, probably reduced the economic incentive to immigrate, because potential immigrants would expect that it would be very difficult to find employment.

4.   The reduction in the annualized cost of migration would lead to more migration (the number of migrants would be greater than 20 million). In the new equilibrium, with a smaller gap (c), the wage rate after migration would be greater than $3.20 in the South, and less than $5.00 in the North. Each of the areas of gain and loss (a, b, d, e, and f) would be larger.

6.   If we count immigrants as part of the United States even before they move, then before migration the nation as a whole has 142 million people of working age, the total income is $6,917,340 million (= 6,909,840 + 7,500), and the average income is $48,714. With this consistent treatment of the immigrants, immigration increases both the average and the total income of the United States. The United States as the receiving country and the immigrants themselves gain from immigration.

8.   This statement is probably false. The migrants do improve their economic well-being. But once they leave they are no longer part of the sending country. The sending country can lose in two ways. First, analysis of the labor-market effects of emigration indicates that, while workers remaining in the sending country gain, employers and others in the sending country lose more, so the net effect on the sending country is a loss. Second, the

net fiscal effect of emigration is probably a loss for the sending country. The emigrants have often received education paid for by the government, but the emigrants shift to paying taxes to the receiving-country government once they leave. We should also note one major way that the sending country can gain—emigrants often send back remittances to relatives and friends. The overall effect on the sending country is then unclear, but a loss is likely in many cases.

10.   Here are several arguments. First, Japan is already a crowded place, with many Japanese living in densely populated metropolitan areas (especially Tokyo). Allowing more immigrants will add to the external costs of congestion, because most immigrants will want to live and work in urban areas. Second, increased immigration will add to social frictions. It will not be easy to change Japanese attitudes against foreigners. Instead, the immigrants are likely to face substantial discrimination based on prejudice. Japan's policy must be decided with this reality in mind. Third, the immigrants easily could be a net fiscal burden. If the policy is not suitably selective, Japan will receive many immigrants who have little education and low labor skills. These immigrants will pay low taxes, but they will receive substantial benefits from Japanese government programs, including government-financed medical care. Fourth, the native groups that will lose from increased immigration include lower skilled Japanese workers who already have low earnings. The Japanese government should not institute a policy change that harms the least well off within the country, even if it might bring net gains to the country overall.

Chapter 26

International Lending and Financial Crises

Overview

International capital movements can bring major gains both to the lending or investing countries and to the borrowing countries, through intertemporal trade and through portfolio diversification for the lenders/investors. But international lending and borrowing is not always well-behaved—financial crises are recurrent. This chapter examines both the gains from well-behaved lending and borrowing and what we know about international financial crises.

We begin with the economic analysis of international capital flows that focuses on the stock of wealth of two countries and how that wealth can be lent or invested in the two countries. With no international lending, the country that has much wealth relative to its domestic investment opportunities will have a lower rate of return or interest rate. Freeing international capital flows permits the low-rate country to lend to the high-rate country. As the world shifts to an equilibrium with free capital movements, both countries gain. As usual, however, within each country there are groups that gain and groups that lose from the international lending.

We can also use this analysis to show that either nation could gain from imposing a small tax on the international capital flows, because it could shift the pre-tax foreign interest rate in its favor. Either country could seek to impose a nationally optimal tax, but this works well only if the other country does not impose a comparable tax.

International lending and borrowing between industrialized countries generally is well-behaved, but this is not the case for lending by industrialized countries to developing countries. The chapter provides a tour of the history of this latter kind of lending from the 1970s to the late 1990s. Following defaults in the 1930s, lending to developing countries was low for four decades. Such lending dramatically increased in the 1970s for four reasons. First, oil-exporting countries deposited large amounts of petrodollars in banks following the increases in oil prices. Second, the banks did not see good prospects for lending this money to borrowers for capital spending in the industrialized countries. Third, developing countries resisted direct foreign investment from multinationals based in the industrialized countries, so increased capital flows to the developing countries took the form of bank loans to these countries. Fourth, herd behavior among banks increased the total amount lent to developing countries.

Crisis struck in 1982, when first Mexico and then many other developing countries declared that they could not repay. The crisis was brought on by rising interest rates in the United States, which raised the cost of servicing the loans, and declining export earnings for the debtor developing countries, as the industrialized countries endured a deep recession. This debt crisis wore on through the 1980s. Beginning in 1989, the Brady Plan led to reductions in debt and conversion to bonds. By 1994, the 1980s debt crisis was finally over.

Beginning in about 1990 lending to developing countries began to grow rapidly. Low U.S. interest rates led lenders and investors to seek out better returns elsewhere, and many developing countries became more attractive as places to invest by shifting to more market-oriented policies. In addition, individual investors and fund managers began to view developing countries as emerging markets for financial investments.

Still, the 1990s were punctuated by a series of financial crises. In late 1994 a large current account deficit, a weak banking system, and rapid growth in dollar-indexed Mexican government debt (*tesobonos*) led to a large devaluation and depreciation of the Mexican peso and a financial crisis as foreign investors refused to buy new *tesobonos*. Contagion (the "tequila effect") spread the crisis to other countries. A large rescue package offered mostly by the U.S. government and the International Monetary Fund (IMF) contained the crisis and the contagion.

The Asian crisis of 1997 hit Thailand first and then spread to Indonesia and South Korea, as well as Malaysia and the Philippines. The problems differed somewhat from one country to another, but one cause of the crisis was weak government regulation of banks, so that the banks borrowed large amounts of foreign currency, and then lent these funds to risky local borrowers. In addition, the growth of exports generally was declining for these countries, leading to some weakness in the current account.

Russia was not much affected directly by the Asian crisis, but it had a large fiscal deficit and the need for large borrowing by the government. By mid-1998 foreign lenders reduced their financing, and an IMF loan foundered when the Russian government failed to enact changes in its fiscal policy. In the face of rising capital flight, the Russian crisis hit, as the Russian government allowed the ruble to depreciate and defaulted on much of its debt. With no rescue from the IMF, foreign lenders and investors suffered large losses. They reassessed the risk of lending to developing countries, and flows of capital to developing countries declined for the year. A small crisis hit Brazil in early 1999, as the real was floated and immediately depreciated by a large amount.

Based on a survey of recent studies of financial crises, the chapter discusses five reasons why they occur or are as severe as they are. The explanations have a common theme—once foreign lenders realize that there is a problem, each has incentive to stop lending and to try to get repaid as quickly as possible. If the borrower cannot immediately repay, a crisis occurs. The first explanation is overlending and overborrowing. This can occur when the government borrows and guarantees private borrowing, and lenders view this as low risk. The box on "The Special Case of Sovereign Debt" uses a benefit-cost analysis to show when a sovereign debtor would default. The Asian crisis showed that overlending and overborrowing could occur with private borrowers as well, especially if rising stock and land prices show high returns until the bubble bursts. The second explanation is exogenous shocks—for instance, a decline in export prices or a rise in foreign (often U.S.) interest rates—that make it more difficult for the borrower to service its debt. The third is exchange rate risk. This can be acute if private borrowers use liabilities denominated in foreign currency to fund assets denominated in local currency, betting that the exchange rate value of the local currency will not decline (too much). If it does, borrowers attempt to hedge their risk exposure, putting further downward pressure on the exchange-rate value of the local currency, and then may be forced to default if the local currency is depreciated or devalued more, before they can fully hedge their risk exposures. The fourth explanation is a large increase in short-term debt to foreigners. The risk is that short-term debt denominated in foreign currency cannot readily be rolled over or refinanced.

The first four explanations indicate why a financial crisis can hit a country. The fifth explanation—global contagion—indicates why a crisis in one country can spread to others. Contagion can be herding behavior, perhaps fed partly by incomplete information on other countries that might have problems similar to those of the crisis country. Contagion can also be based on a new recognition of real problems in other countries, with the crisis in the first country serving as a "wake-up call."

When a financial crisis hits, two major types of international efforts are used to help resolve it. First, a rescue package, often led by an IMF lending facility, can be used to compensate temporarily for the lack of private lending, to try to restore lender confidence, to try to limit contagion, and to induce the government of the borrowing country to improve its macroeconomic and other policies. While the Mexican rescue in 1994 was very successful in helping Mexico weather the crisis, the rescue packages for the Asian crisis countries were only moderately successful. A key question is whether the rescue packages increase moral hazard, so that future financial crises become more likely because lenders lend more freely if they expect to be rescued. The Mexican rescue probably increased moral hazard, with mixed effects from the Asian rescues. The lack of a rescue for Russia reduced moral hazard as lenders lost substantial amounts with no rescue package implemented.

Second, debt restructuring (rescheduling and reduction) is used to create a more manageable stream of payments for debt service. Restructuring can be difficult because an individual lender has an incentive to free ride, hoping that other creditors will restructure while demanding full repayment as quickly as possible for its own loans. The Brady Plan overcame the free rider problems to resolve the debt crisis of the 1980s. During the debt crises of the 1990s, it has been relatively easy to restructure debt owed to foreign banks. The new problem is the great difficulty of restructuring bonds, because the legal terms of most bonds gives powers to small numbers of bondholders to resist restructuring.

We now are paying more attention to finding ways to reduce the likelihood or frequency of financial crises. Some proposals for improved practices in borrowing countries, including better macroeconomic policies, better disclosure of information and data, avoiding government short-term borrowing denominated in foreign currencies, and better regulation of banks, enjoy widespread support. Other proposals are controversial, with experts sometimes pointing in opposite directions. Developing countries should shift to relatively cleanly floating exchange rates, or they should move to rigid currency fixes through currency boards. The IMF should have access to greater amounts of resources so it can help countries fight off unwarranted financial attacks, or the IMF should be abolished to reduce moral hazard. The chapter concludes by looking more closely at two proposals for reform, the need for better bank regulation, and the controversial proposal that developing countries should make greater use of capital controls to limit capital inflows, and especially to limit short-term borrowing.

Tips

Many students have a keen interest in international lending and investing and in the financial crises that have hit in the 1990s. This chapter, like some others, can readily be supplemented with readings from the recent press, using articles on the aftermath of recent crises and on new crises (e.g., Ecuador's default on Brady bonds in late 1999).

The first section or two of this chapter on the gains from international capital flows and the taxation of international capital flows can be assigned and covered in conjunction with the material of Part I, Part II, the labor-market migration analysis of Chapter 25, or the analysis of direct investment in Chapter 27.

Suggested answers to questions and problems
(in the textbook)

2.   Disagree. In a sense a national government cannot go bankrupt, because it can print its own currency. But a national government can refuse to honor its obligations, even if it might be able to pay. If the benefit from not paying exceeds the cost of not paying, the government may rationally refuse to pay. And, a national government can run short of foreign currency to pay obligations denominated in foreign currency, because it cannot print foreign money.

4.   The debt crisis in 1982 was precipitated by (a) increased cost of servicing debt, because of a rise in interest rates in the United States and other developed countries as tighter monetary policies were used to fight inflation, (b) decreased export earnings in the debtor countries, because of decreased demand and lower commodity prices as the tighter monetary policies resulted in a world recession, and (c) an investor stampede to curtail new lending and get old loans repaid quickly, once it became clear that (a) and (b) would lead to some defaults.

6.   With free international lending Japan lends 1,800 (= 6,000 - 4,200) to America, at point T. If Japan and America each impose a 2 percent tax on international lending, the total tax is 4 percent. The gap WZ restores equilibrium, and the amount lent internationally declines to 600 (= 6,000 - 5,400). The interest rate in Japan (and the one received net of taxes by Japan's international lenders) is 3 percent and the interest rate in America (and the one paid including taxes by America's international borrowers) is 7 percent. (The difference is the 4 percent of taxes.) Japan's government collects international-lending tax revenues equal to area r, but this is effectively paid by Japanese lenders who see their earnings on the 600 of foreign lending that continues decline by this amount. The net effect on Japan is a loss of area n because the taxes prevent some previously profitable lending from occurring. America's government collects tax revenues equal to area k, but

this is effectively paid by American borrowers who must pay a higher interest rate on their foreign borrowing. The net effect on America is a loss of area j because of the decline in international borrowing.

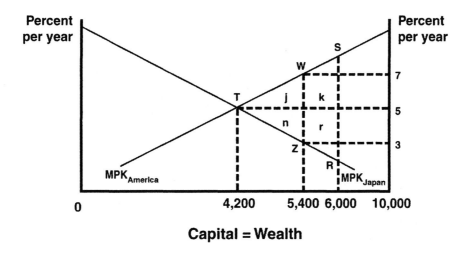

8. a. The increase in the interest rate rotates the line showing the debt service due, which is also the benefit from not repaying, upward to $(1 + i')D$ from $(1 + i)D$. The threshold amount of debt beyond which the country's government should default declines to D_{lim}' from D_{lim}. This change can lead to default, even if the country's government would not default before the change, if the actual amount of debt is between D_{lim}' and D_{lim}.

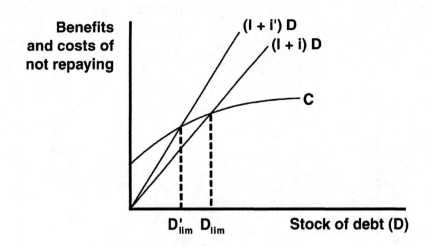

b.   The increase in the cost of defaulting causes an upward shift to C′ from C in the curve showing the costs of not repaying. In this case the threshold increases to $D_{lim}′$ from D_{lim}. This change cannot lead to default if the country would not default before the change.

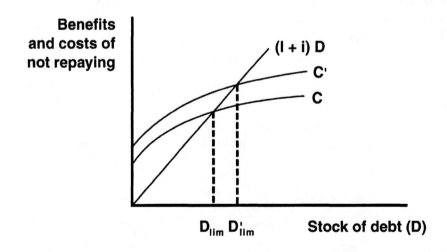

10.   If a default has no other effect on Puglia, its government should default when the cost of servicing the debt (interest paid plus repayment of principal) is larger than the inflow of funds. This occurs at the end of year 3, so the Puglian government should default at that time.

Chapter 27

Direct Foreign Investment and the Multinationals

Overview

This chapter provides a survey of the economics of direct foreign investment. Direct foreign investment (DFI) is a flow of lending to, or purchases of ownership in, a foreign enterprise by the investing-country resident(s) (usually firm(s)) that own and exert management control of the foreign enterprise. The minimum amount of ownership that is considered to be necessary to have sufficient management control varies from country to country—the United States uses 10 percent ownership in its official definition. (DFI may also refer to the stock of such investments in existence at a point in time.)

To understand DFI we must recognize that it is more than just a capital movement. The foreign affiliate (subsidiary or branch) often receives managerial skills and methods, technology and trade secrets, marketing capabilities and brand names, and instructions about business practices from its parent company. Often much of the financing of the affiliate is raised locally, perhaps to reduce exposure to exchange rate risk or to the risk of expropriation by the host-country government.

Industrialized countries are the source of most DFI, and most DFI goes into industrialized countries (although recently the share going to developing countries has risen). Direct investment is more important in some industries than in others. In manufacturing DFI is important in such industries as chemicals, electrical and electronic products, automobiles, machinery, and food. In services DFI is important in such activities as financial services, business services, and wholesaling and retailing.

What explains DFI? Purely financial theories cannot explain DFI because they cannot explain why managerial control over the foreign affiliates, with its focus on production and marketing, is necessary if the goal is only to move capital from one country to another in pursuit of higher returns or diversification of risk. DFI also does not seem to be the accidental outcome of perfect competition, because firms face inherent disadvantages in operating affiliates in foreign countries. To overcome the disadvantages and to be successful with its DFI, a firm must have some firm-specific advantages not held by its local competitors in the foreign country. These advantages may be technologies, marketing assets, managerial capabilities, or access to large amounts of financial capital.

These firm-specific advantages indicate that imperfect competition is likely to be important in understanding DFI. The Hymer view is that DFI is used to stifle competition and enhance the market power of the multinational firms. If this is true, then host government policies that limit or regulate DFI can be in the national interest. The appropriability theory emphasizes that firms must make investments to develop and maintain any firm-specific advantages. DFI is part of the competitive effort to earn returns on these investments—DFI is often the best way to appropriate (capture) the potential gains from the advantages. If this is true, then the firm-specific advantages are valuable productive resources, and host government policies might best be neutral toward DFI or positively encourage it.

The taxation of the profits of multinational firms raises important issues. Although the details are overwhelming, the general approach to how the profits are taxed is that the profits of the foreign affiliates are taxed by the host country and the profits of the parent company on its own activities are taxed by the home country. To minimize total taxes paid worldwide, multinationals can try to locate activities in low-tax countries. More controversially, multinational firms can use transfer pricing on transactions that occur within the global organization to show more of their profits in countries where they will be lightly taxed. Governments know this incentive. They often attempt to police transfer pricing to assure that transfer prices are similar to market prices, but this determination is often difficult, so the firms have some scope to manipulate transfer pricing.

Multinational firms are active in international trade in goods and services, and about one-third of world trade is intra-firm trade between units of multinational firms in different countries. Although some DFI is a substitute for trade, because local production replaces products that otherwise would be imported, DFI and trade are also often complements. This is especially true when multinational firms exploit differences in comparative advantages by locating different stages of production in different countries. It can also be true when better local marketing by an affiliate leads to increased sales of some products that the multinational firm produces in other countries, even if other parts of the firm's product line are produced locally by the affiliate. Most studies conclude that DFI overall is somewhat complementary to international trade in products.

Economic analysis suggests that the home (or source) country overall benefits from its outward DFI, as long as the profits earned on the foreign investments count as part of the country's benefit. Some groups in the home country, including labor, are likely to be harmed. There are some arguments for the home country to tax or restrict outward DFI. The multinationals' profits may not be viewed as part of the national benefit, or the multinationals may gain too much influence over the country's foreign policies. The home country could gain from an optimal tax on the DFI, or positive externalities may be lost when the activities are shifted out of the country. The policies of the major home countries are neutral to mildly supportive toward outward DFI.

Economic analysis suggests that the host country also gains from inward DFI, even if the profits of the local affiliates do not belong to the host country, and even though some local competitors may be harmed by the competition from the affiliates. There is some case for the host-country government to tax or restrict inward DFI, because of fear of the local political power of the foreign multinationals, or to impose an optimal tax on the affiliate's profits. But the DFI may also bring technological spillovers and other positive externalities. Since the mid-1970s host countries have generally been liberalizing their policies toward inward DFI, and many actively compete for it by offering various forms of subsidies to multinational firms that will locate new facilities in their countries.

Tips

Figure 27.1 has quite a bit of information that can be used to generate class discussion, including the identity of the major home countries (why these are the major home countries?), the relatively small amount of DFI into developing countries and more generally what countries and regions host most DFI (why?), and the specific pattern of DFI for each home country (why?).

Suggested answers to questions and problems
(in the textbook)

2.   Disagree. Industrialized countries do have large amounts of financial capital that they want to invest. Even if they want to invest part of this capital in other countries, this does not explain why they are the source of most direct foreign investment. If the goal is only to invest financial capital in other countries, then the easier way to do this is through portfolio investments in foreign stocks, bonds, and loans. Direct foreign investment also involves a transfer of technology, marketing skills, managerial capabilities, and other firm-specific assets to the foreign subsidiary, and these are often more important than the financial investment in the subsidiary. Industrialized countries are the source of most DFI because firms based in these countries have developed these intangible assets, which then serve as the base for successful DFI.

4.   We can guess that there are two possible types of reasons. One is that Japan is not attractive as a host country, based on its economic and business characteristics. The second is that Japanese government policy artificially limits DFI into Japan. First, the low level of DFI into Japan could be the result of economic and business conditions. Foreign firms may find Japan a difficult place in which to establish a business, because Japanese practices and procedures are different and difficult to learn about. Cultural and language differences make foreign management more difficult and more prone to misunderstandings and mistakes. Foreign firms also may find that Japan is a relatively expensive place to run a business, because of the high cost of land, the difficulty of hiring experienced skilled labor (given "lifetime employment" at established large Japanese companies), and the strong exchange rate value of the yen since the mid-1980s. Second, the low level of DFI into Japan could be the result of Japanese government policies. Until the late 1960s to mid-1970s, Japanese government policies explicitly prevented direct investment into Japan. Since then, foreign firms may be deterred by more subtle governmental barriers, including the tendency of the Japanese government to find ways to favor its own firms. In addition, the Japanese government imposes a large amount of regulation which tends to deter entry into business by both new Japanese firms and foreign firms. Probably, both of these reasons are of some importance in explaining why Japan is host to rather little direct investment, but there is controversy over which one is more important.

6. a.   Not DFI, assuming that the U.S. investor ends up owning less than 10 percent of the outstanding shares of Volkswagen.

    b.   DFI. A flow of lending to a foreign enterprise that is more than 10 percent owned by the U.S. firm providing the loan.

    c.   DFI. Additional purchases of ownership of a foreign enterprise by the U.S. investor that then owns more than 10 percent of the foreign enterprise.

    d.   The $100,000 is DFI, because the Brazilian affiliate is owned by the U.S. firm. The loan from the Brazilian bank is not DFI if it is made to the Brazilian affiliate.

8.   Labor groups seek restrictions on the flow of direct investment out of the United States because outward DFI tends to lower labor income. This reduction may occur for three major reasons. First, the DFI is shifting jobs out of the United States, so some U.S. workers lose as they become unemployed. Second, the general decrease in demand for labor puts downward pressure on wage rates. Third, the bargaining power of unionized labor is reduced when companies can threaten to shift production out of the United States. Unions cannot bargain so effectively to gain higher wages. Standard economic analysis shows that the losses to labor are more than offset by the gains to the owners of the companies undertaking the DFI. This standard analysis suggests that labor is mainly defending its special interest. But, there may be problems with the standard analysis. Most important, are the multinational firms' owners actually part of the United States? These owners may be from many countries, or they may not be viewed as being sufficiently tied to the United States. If much of what is gained by the owners of the multinational firms is not counted as a gain to the United States, then the losses to U.S. labor are not countered by gains elsewhere in the country. In this case the opposition of U.S. labor to outward DFI may also be in the national interest.

10.   Key points that should be included in the report:
(1) DFI brings new technologies into the country.
(2) DFI brings new managerial practices into the country.
(3) DFI brings marketing capabilities into the country. These can be used to better meet the needs of the local market. They may be particularly important in expanding the country's exports by improving the international marketing of products produced by the multinational firms that begin production in the country.
(4) DFI brings financial capital into the country, and expands the country's ability to invest in domestic production capabilities.
(5) The local affiliates of the multinationals raise labor skills by training local workers.
(6) Other technological (and similar) side benefits accrue to the country as it hosts DFI, because some of the multinationals' technology, managerial practices, and marketing capabilities spread to local firms as they learn about and imitate the multinational's intangible assets. Taken together, these first six items serve to increase the country's supply-side capabilities for producing (and selling) goods and services.
(7) In addition, the country's government can gain additional tax revenues by taxing (in a reasonable way!) the profits of the local affiliates established by the foreign multinationals.